Advance Praise for

The Dog Lover's Book of Crafts

"Is your creativity looking for a good home? Jennifer Quasha's new book is full of useful and attractive crafts for a dog lover to make, with easy-to-follow instructions and illustrations. So sit, stay, and create!"　—MARK BRICKLIN, author of *Pets' Letters to God*

"*The Dog Lover's Book of Crafts* is a wonderful collection of beautiful and unique items designed for both the artist and dog lover in you. Jennifer Quasha's love of dogs and her creativity shine all the way through this tastefully illustrated book. The step-by-step instructions make it simple for us dog lovers to produce distinctive decorations sure to bring a smile to whoever sets eyes on them."—STEVE DILLER, author of *Dogs and Their People*

"Clearly a huge dog lover, Jennifer Quasha has come up with a terrific collection of home decorations that belong in every dog-loving household—with the added bonus that even the dog can help create them."　—AMANDA WAKELEY, fashion designer

"As *le connaisseur de la vie du chien,* Monsieur would like to congratulate Mademoi-selle Quasha on her fabulous book of crafts. It's high time that someone recognized the fine art of decoupage. *Merci!* One must always create, especially when inspired by one's *chien* (dog)!"
　　—ELIZABETH ELKINS AND MONSIEUR JEAN LAFITTE, authors of the *Jean Lafitte International Series*

"Jennifer Quasha has come up with a fantastic idea for a book that is clever and easy and amusing, with amazing detail. Waste no time, take the dog with you, and run out to buy it immediately."
　　—KELLY HOPPEN, interior designer and author of *East Meet West, In Touch, Table Chic* and *Close Up*

"Great! The only problem is I can't decide whether I should start by making a Rex silhouette or a Rex placemat."
　　—VALERIE SHAFF, photographer and coauthor of *If You Only Knew How Much I Smelled You, I Am Puppy, Hear Me Yap,* and mother of Rex

"Sammy (the dog) and I are grateful to have the wonderful and informative *Dog Lover's Book of Crafts* as it will add class and elegance to our lives."
　　　　—ELLIOTT ERWITT, photographer and author of *Dog Dogs*

"This is the perfect book for the consummate dog lover who's about to go around the bend."
　　—KITTY HAWKS, president and co-founder of Tails In Need, Inc., and co-chairwoman of The Great American Mutt Show

"This is the greatest thing since sliced dog food."　—A-DIFFICULT-TO-PLEASE NEW YORK EDITOR

The Dog Lover's
Book of Crafts

JENNIFER QUASHA

The Dog Lover's Book of Crafts

Home Decorations That Celebrate Man's Best Friend

St. Martin's Griffin ❧ New York

THE DOG LOVER'S BOOK OF CRAFTS. Copyright © 2002 by Jennifer Quasha.
All rights reserved. Printed in the United States of America.
No part of this book may be used or reproduced in any manner whatsoever
without written permission except in the case of brief quotations
embodied in critical articles or reviews.
For information, address St. Martin's Press,
175 Fifth Avenue, New York, N.Y. 10010.

www.stmartins.com

www.dogloverscrafts.com

Illustrations by Georg Brewer

Book design by Kate Nichols

LIBRARY OF CONGRESS CATALOGING-IN-PUBLICATION DATA

Quasha, Jennifer.
    The dog lover's book of crafts : 50 home decorations that celebrate man's best friend /
Jennifer Quasha.—1st ed.
        p. cm.
    ISBN 0-312-28234-6
    1. Dogs—Equipment and supplies. 2. Handicraft. 3. Decoration and ornament. I. Title.
SF427.15.Q37 2001
745.5—dc21   2001041964

First Edition: December 2001

1 2 3 4 5 6 7 8 9 10

For Ted,

my best two-legged friend,

and Scout,

my best four-legged friend

Contents

Introduction: On Being a Dog-Loving Crafter or
  a Craft-Loving Dog Person   xiii

About This Book   xv

PART ONE
Doggie-Chic Interior Design: Home Decor Starring Your Dog

1.	Fido Finials	3
2.	Wipe Your Paws! Doormat	5
3.	Bone Doormat	6
4.	Retriever Message Board	7
5.	The Tassel That Wags the Dog	10
6.	Fetch, Run, Catch, Play! Tic-Tac-Toe Board	13
7.	Our Doghouse Placard	15
8.	Kanine Key Hooks	17
9.	Dogs-in-Art Tissue Box Cover	20
10.	Dog Run Corkboard	22
11.	Bone Bales	25

PART TWO
All Paws on the Table:
Tabletop Decorations Featuring Fido and His Friends

12.	Lyin' Dog Place Card Holders	29
13.	Mug-for-Me Decoupage Plates	32
14.	Give-a-Dog-a-Bone Place Mats	35
15.	Dog Phrase Napkin Rings	37
16.	No-Drool Napkins	39
17.	Lucky's Luminary	42
18.	Paw Print Magnets	46
19.	Poochie-Poo Pitcher Protector	49
20.	Best-in-Show Lazy Susan	51

PART THREE
How Much Is That Doggie in the Window?
Picture Frames for Your Furry Friend

21.	Dog Tag Picture Frame	57
22.	A Frame Good Enough to Eat	59
23.	Pet Silhouette	61
24.	Playing Pooches Frame	65
25.	All-About-Dogs Decoupage Picture Frame	67

PART FOUR
Get on the Couch!
Pooch Pillows and Other Stuffed Stuff

	Pillow Talk: The Basics	71
26.	Pugs & Pillows	72
27.	Royal Pug Pillows	75
28.	Hugo's Dog-Bone Button Pillow	78
29.	My Baby's Name in Bones	82
30.	Scottie Pillowcase	84
31.	Your-Dog-Here Pillow	88

Doggie Sachets 92

32. Bundle Sachet 93

33. Shaped Sachet 95

34. Single Breed Sachet 96

35. Antique Dog-Button Pillow 98

PART FIVE
Paper Training for Humans:
Woofer Wrappings and Supplies

36. Sammy Stamps 103

37. Bone and Hydrant Sponge Stamps 106

38. Who Let the Dogs Out? Stencils 108

39. Tail-Waggingly Easy Invitation 110

40. Woofer Wrapping Paper and Gift Tags 113

41. "Pup-Up" Invitation or Greeting Card 116

42. Ode to Toupee Drink Coasters 120

PART SIX
The Holidays Have Gone to the Dogs:
Festive Fido Decorations

43. A Holiday Dog Breed Ornament 125

44. Too-Proud-to-Beg Bone Ornament 128

45. Kennel Klub Kristmas Ornaments 130

46. Paw Print Ornament 133

PART SEVEN
Putting on the Pooch:
For Dog Lovers on the Move

47. A-OK Dog Tag Earrings 137

48. Dog-Button Earrings and Brooch 139

49. Sighing Dog Brooches 141

50. Dog-Chase Garden Hat 144

Appendix A: Top Dog Breeds   147

Appendix B: Tracing Outlines of the Top 50 Dog Breeds   149

Appendix C: Listing and Images of Selected Dog Breeds
   and Related Craft Projects   159

Sources   167

Acknowledgments   171

Index   173

Introduction:
On Being a Dog-Loving Crafter or
a Craft-Loving Dog Person

When I was six years old my parents decided to get me, their only child, a puppy. After research it was resolved that an English Springer Spaniel was just the exuberant breed for their exuberant child. It was a wise choice; however, the name given to this pooch was less so. I wanted to name her Jill after my aunt, but Mom and Dad vetoed that one the second it came out of my mouth. So after much thought (for a six-year-old), I came up with Fluffy for our new flat-coated, unfluffy puppy.

So began my love of dogs. Fluffy was never "just a dog"; she was utterly and completely my sibling. Fluff and I coexisted in the life that I led outside of school. She was looking up at me when I opened my eyes in the morning, she was sitting by the door when I came home from school, and she was lying on my bed every night when I turned out the light. We played dress up and hide-and-seek, had tea parties for two, swam together in the pool, and waded in the brook out back. Fluffy remained by my side throughout my parents' parting of ways and those uncomfortable middle-school years when I felt like I didn't fit in anywhere. Even when we moved from one continent to another, Fluffy was still there.

Other breeds and other dogs have followed in Fluffy's paw prints, and they have all been terrific in their own way. Each has had his or her own personality, and not a single one of the eight Bichon Frises that my family has brought into our home has been alike. Their gaits, mugs, fur, eyes, reactions, allergies, food preferences, and lounging positions are all varied, and every one of them provided me, and some still do, much laughter and joy. Today, Scout, my very own long-legged, mischievous Bichon, has me wrapped around his nonopposable thumb.

Along with the hours spent with Fluff in my youth, my mother and I spent a lot of time making stuff. I learned how to use a sewing machine at age eight, and if the machine was not clacking away while her hands guided through my latest Halloween costume, it was clacking away as I steered through my six hundredth, poly-filled pillow. I was knitting sweaters with different-length sleeves, needlepointing yet another colorful brick cover, painting some really bad art, sawing whale-shaped cutting boards for anyone who wanted one, and many other unmentionables. In school, art was always my favorite subject. Since then I have painted and drawn, knit and stitched, embroidered and glued, sanded and nailed. I have found no other way to visit that peaceful place where crafting takes me.

About This Book

It has been one of my greatest pleasures to write this book. It is my small hope that whoever reads this book gets one-tenth as much joy from celebrating both dogs and crafts as I do. I tried to vary the breeds I used in each craft to show you that any dog can be the star. You can use your favorite dogs throughout your projects or make a project for your friends and family starring their dogs.

I have tried to make this book as user-friendly as possible. Here's how:

These crafts are all easy. It is simply a matter of how much time you want to spend crafting. The message board might take a day or two, and the lamp finials will take about ten minutes.

You can find all the tools and materials you need to use easily. All the craft supplies I use can be found in craft stores or other stores like a lighting, lamp, or fabric store. In the back of the book is a Sources section that lists phone numbers, addresses, and Web sites for everything I used. Also in the back of the book are tracing outlines of the fifty most popular breeds, which you can photocopy or trace to help you in many of the crafts (see Appendix B on page 149).

Hints and tips are provided throughout the book. Along with Georg Brewer's fabulous step-by-step illustrations, I have added suggestions in the Hints & Tips section so that you don't make the same mistakes I did. Read them *before* you start the craft. Also, I have included a Dog-Difficulty Scale to rate the craft against the others in the book. You can find it next to the Hints & Tips in every craft.

DOG-DIFFICULTY SCALE

 An Easy Trick

 Easy with Some Practice

 Might Take Some Training

You don't need to spend a lot of money.
As with most things in life, there's a range of how much to spend. For example, you can buy doggie fabric for $8 a yard or for $128 a yard. However, it is up to you how much you want to spend. None of these crafts will ask you to shell out a lot of money. For example, in the pillow crafts, you can use plain buttons that are sold ten for a dollar or antique brass buttons that cost ten dollars each. It's up to you.

If I have a second to spare while I race around my hometown of New York City, I let myself go gaga over every dog I see. Big or small, with long hair or short fur, drooler or nondrooler, I love them all. Connecting, even for a moment, with a dog reminds me of why all dogs are so special. My Aunt Susie asked me recently as I was cooing over Brewster, her Shih Tzu, "Jenny, do you really love *all* dogs?" It was as easy for me to say yes to that question as it is for a well-treated dog to come up to a total stranger and, for no reason at all, lick them.

Enjoy!

Doggie-Chic
Interior Design

Home Decor

Starring Your Dog

Fido Finials

Give a plain lamp a small decorative touch by adding some interest to the finial. (Finials are those little knobs that hold the lamp shade to the frame of the lamp.) Some lamps come with decorative finials already, but most don't. Although this is probably the easiest craft in the book, when it's complete, it looks the least homemade.

If you don't already have a pair of plain, slightly-rounded-top finials, they are easy to find. Most lamp stores carry a variety of finials since, when moving house, finials often go missing. The finials you want to buy have a slightly rounded top and are usually the least expensive ones. At my local lamp store in New York City they sell these finials for twenty-five cents each, and this is New York City. (My mom's lamp-store guy gives her hers for free.) These ceramic dogs I bought at a toy store, but I have also seen them in old-fashioned general stores and craft stores. You can also use wooden and plastic creatures, so keep your eyes open wherever you shop.

Difficulty Rating:

TOOLS & MATERIALS

✔ Hammer
✔ 2 finials
✔ Strong household glue
✔ 2 miniature dog figures

Step-by-Step Directions

1. If necessary, using the hammer, flatten the slightly rounded top of the two finials.

2. Place a dab of glue onto the top of the finial.

3. Glue on one of the dog figurines.

4. Repeat for second finial.

Hints & Tips

- Unless the figurine is very small, choose a dog that is seated or lying down so most of the figurine will be in contact with the finial. Gluing only one or two paws to the finial probably will not make it sturdy enough.
- Since you are using a strong adhesive, use less glue than you originally might want to. Excess glue will ooze from between the figurine and finial and will not look as good.
- Do not worry if the two finials you find at the lamp store are not exactly the same. You won't notice the difference.
- The dogs do not have to match either! Choose two different dogs, but if they are for the same pair of lamps, keep them about the same size.
- When buying the ceramic dogs, keep the lamp you will be using in mind. You do not want a large figurine on top of a small lamp, or a teeny dog on top of a huge lamp.

> **BREEDOIDS: 1. Dachshund** means "badger dog" in German: The breed was trained to follow badgers, foxes, and rabbits into the ground. **2. Basset Hounds** are descendants of the French St. Hubert dogs and *bas* in French means "low." **3. English Springer Spaniels** were named because they crouch low to the ground and then spring forward toward their prey.

Quote

"Dachshunds are ideal dogs for children, as they are already stretched and pulled to such a length that the child cannot do much harm one way or another."
—Robert Benchley

Wipe Your Paws! Doormat

Even though I live in an apartment building in New York City and as I come in off the street my feet trod on my building's foyer carpet, the rug in the elevator, the rug in the hallway, and my very own Wipe Your Paws! mat, I still manage to track in water, soot, and dirt. Sometimes, on particularly wet and grimy days, I even wipe Scout's paws for him on the mat. Although it pleases him a lot less than it pleases me to gaze down at my homemade mat, I figure it's much more tolerable for

him than a bath. These mats are so easy to make and making one is a fun way to spend an hour or so on the weekend. They also make terrific housewarming gifts or welcome-to-the-neighborhood thoughts for the people who just moved in next door.

Difficulty Rating:

TOOLS & MATERIALS

✔ 1" polyester paintbrush
✔ Coir doormat
✔ White chalk
✔ Hunter green enamel paint
✔ Flathead screwdriver

Step-by-Step Directions

1. Using the chalk, sketch your design into the mat.

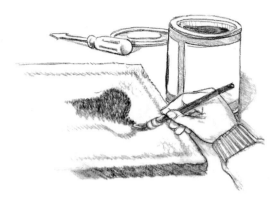

2. After opening the can of paint with the screwdriver, dip the tip of the brush into the paint, and dab paint onto the mat, following your design.

3. Repeat twice, and let dry overnight.

Hints & Tips

- You want as much paint as possible to sink down into the coir, so don't use paint strokes. Try dabbing instead.
- Use a lot of paint. I dipped my brush into the paint after every dab.

- Use a cheap brush so you can just throw it away after the project is complete.
- Since dabbing the paint around the mat takes time, there is no need to wait and let the paint dry before adding the next coat.

Bone Doormat

Substitute your favorite color or favorite doggie item and create your own unique mat, following the directions for making Wipe Your Paws! Doormats on page 5. Try various borders or use a small brush and paint little bones all over the mat. Also think about making a mat using two different paint colors.

> **BREEDOIDS: 1.** The **Chesapeake Bay Retriever** is Maryland's state dog. **2.** Despite its name, the **Australian Shepherd** probably came from the Pyrenees Mountains, which lie between Spain and France.

Retriever Message Board

These message boards are sold all over, but it's easy to make your own with exactly the fabric you want to use. Between the color and pattern of the fabric, the ribbon, and the color and design of upholstery tacks, yours will be one of a kind. Mine, which has retrievers all over the fabric, hangs to the right of my desk and is filled with postcards and photos, mostly of dogs, of course.

Difficulty Rating:

TOOLS & MATERIALS

✔ 36" x 45" piece of craft batting
✔ 18" x 24" piece of plywood
✔ Staple gun
✔ 26" x 56" of dog-themed fabric
✔ Pins
✔ 6 yards of ⅜" ribbon, like grosgrain
✔ Scissors or pinking shears
✔ Hammer
✔ 50 upholstery tacks

Step-by-Step Directions

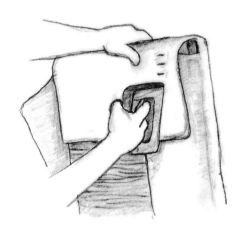

1. Fold the batting in half, cover the front of the plywood, and wrap the remaining batting around to the back of the board. Using the staple gun, staple the batting in place on the back of the plywood.

2. Center the fabric on the front and center of the message board. Turn the board over and, like a gift, wrap the fabric around the batting and plywood, and pin it in place on the back. Turn over the board and make sure that your fabric is centered. If it is, staple gun the fabric in place on the back. If not, correct the fabric before staple gunning it down.

3. Lay and pin the ribbon onto the front of the board, starting with an X in the center of the board.

4. Cut the ribbon into strips, leaving some excess ribbon on each end, and continue working toward the edge of the board, making Xs.

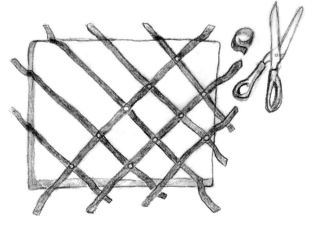

5. Once you have made sure the ribbon Xs are balanced, hammer in upholstery studs to the center of each X on the front. Wrap the remaining ribbon around onto the back of the board and hammer in studs to hold the ends in place.

Hints & Tips

- If you have some extra batting, staple gun it to the back of the board so that the whole board is padded.
- The amount of fabric required for these directions enables you to cover the whole piece of plywood, front and back, with fabric. If you don't care what the back looks like, you only need a piece of fabric that is 26" x 30".
- The reason I suggest having 50 upholstery tacks (even though you need only 25 or so) is that typically half of them bend while being hammered, rendering them useless.
- You can make the craft with only 5 yards of ribbon, but that amount doesn't leave much margin for error.
- You can also use regular tacks on the back of the message board if you run out of upholstery tacks.

- The batting measurement I suggest is also correct if you wanted to use baby-quilt filler, but you can buy other sizes, like strips of it, if the exact measurements listed above are not available.

> **BREEDOIDS: 1. English Springer Spaniels** are one of the most popular hunting dogs because they seem never to tire of running and fetching. **2. Brittanys,** named after the Brittany Province in France, were called Brittany Spaniels until 1982.
>
> **FACTOID:** Not all dogs hunt by smell. **Borzois, Afghans,** and **Salukis** are "gaze hounds," meaning they hunt using their sight.

The Tassel That Wags the Dog

I *have a few friends I can hear saying "I could never do that" when looking at this craft. It really isn't that hard. If you think this craft sounds overwhelming, read the sidebar.*

I love these decorative tassels. I have one small one hanging off each of my lamp switches in the living room and two larger ones hanging off the drawer pulls on my dining-room side table. You can personalize yours by adding a dog figurine.

DOES THIS LOOK TOO TOUGH?

Think of each part of your dog as a separate entity. I think that a dog's hind leg looks a little like a lamb chop. So I mold two miniature lamb chops. The front legs are like two little sticks that are bent at one end to make paws. The tail can be long and straight, short and stubby, or even curled up resting on the dog's back. When creating your dog's head, start with a block of clay. How long or thick is his snout? Does he have a long thin head like a Collie, or is it solid and angular like a Lab? Do her ears flop down to the side like a Springer Spaniel, or stand straight up like a Norwich Terrier? Does the head tilt down on the neck like a Basset Hound, or look up like a Basenji? Are the eyes, nose, and mouth placed closely together on the face, like a Chow or a Pomeranian? Does he look round because of his fur like a Bichon Frise, or is she sleek like a Vizsla or an Italian Greyhound? All these little characteristics, when put together, will help you recognize a particular breed of dog.

TOOLS & MATERIALS

✔ Self-drying clay
✔ Small, narrow paintbrush
✔ Clay tools, or a butter knife
✔ Image of a dog
✔ Bowl of water
✔ Kabob skewer, or something long and thin to poke a hole through the dog's center
✔ Clay sealer
✔ Acrylic paint the color of your dog
✔ 1 decorative tassel

Step-by-Step Directions

1. Using your fingers, the clay tools, or butter knife, mold your dog's head and neck, body, two hind legs, two front legs, and tail with the clay. You want the dog to be about the same size as your tassel, so size accordingly.

2. Connect head and neck, legs, and tail by marking an X on the appropriate place on the dog's body and an X on the part to be attached, and placing a drop of water on one of the Xs.

3. Press together and rub the clay at the place where the two Xs meet so that the seam disappears.

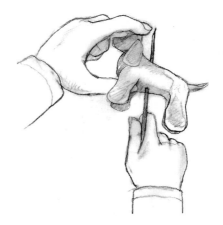

4. When dog is complete, choose a thick area of the dog's body and press the skewer through the clay. Make sure that the hole is big enough for the tassel string to be threaded through. Let the figurine dry.

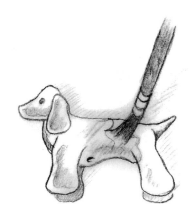

5. Coat with a layer of clay sealer. Let dry.

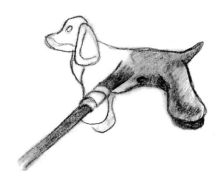

6. Paint the dog and let dry.

7. Thread the tassel through the dog and hang.

Hints & Tips

- Don't make the figure too brittle. For example, if you have a Whippet, it's best to use a bigger tassel so the figurine you make can be bigger too.
- If the pieces you are not working on start to dry out, cover them loosely with plastic wrap. This will keep the clay moist.
- If the figurine is dry and painted and you suddenly realize that the hole through the center of the dog isn't big enough, here's a solution. Cut off a strip of an emery board thin enough to fit into your hole. Gently "sand" the inside of the hole to make it larger.

BREEDOID: How did the **Cocker Spaniel** get its name? Espaignol is French for "Spanish dog," and "Cocker" was used because as early as the fifteenth century the dog was good at chasing woodcocks away.

Fetch, Run, Catch, Play! Tic-Tac-Toe Board

*T*hey sell these tic-tac-toe boards in cata-logs with various props for the Xs and Os, but there is no reason you can't make a doggie version yourself. I considered making the movable pieces dog figures, but I took the easier path and made dog bones and tennis balls. If you are up for making black and yellow seated Labs or adult and puppy versions of the same breed as the movable pieces, it just might be even cuter than this one.

Difficulty Rating:

> **FACTOID:** Exercise is crucial to a dog's health. Depending on the breed, owners should spend close to an hour a day playing with or exercising their dogs.

TOOLS & MATERIALS

- ✔ Self-hardening clay
- ✔ Bowl of water
- ✔ Clay tools, or a butter knife
- ✔ Wax paper
- ✔ Rolling pin, or a round label-free glass bottle
- ✔ Ruler
- ✔ Acrylic paint: red, white, yellow, black
- ✔ Small, narrow, and fine-pointed paintbrush
- ✔ Water-based acrylic glaze

Step-by-Step Directions

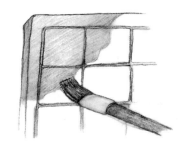

1. Cut off a chunk of clay and place it on a large sheet of wax paper. Cover with another sheet of wax paper and roll flat using a rolling pin. You want to end up with a round piece of clay about ¼" thick and 8" in diameter.

4. Using acrylic paint, paint the clay. Let dry. Coat with acrylic glaze.

Hints & Tips

- Don't let the clay sit on the wax paper for too long as the moisture of the clay dissolves the wax paper, making it stick to the clay.
- Make sure each of your clay tennis balls has a flat area so that it won't roll off the board when it's dry.
- If the clay becomes dry and cracks, use a drop of water to moisten it; it will be easier to work with.

2. Using ruler, measure out a square of clay about 6" to 6½" on each side. Cut out square using the edge of the ruler.

3. Using excess clay, sculpt 5 round balls and 5 bones. Let dry.

BREEDOID: The **Golden Retriever,** the breed that always seems to have a tennis ball in its mouth, was developed in the late nineteenth century by crossing a Retriever and a Tweed Water Spaniel, a dog that is extinct today.

Our Doghouse Placard

I've spent years in the doghouse and it's not such a bad place to be. In fact, our house is a doghouse, and will likely be until it's time to go to dog heaven (which is where I hope I'll end up). This placard will look great hanging from any doorknob, and you can always create your own motto if "Our Doghouse" isn't yours.

Difficulty Rating:

TOOLS & MATERIALS

✔ 5" x 7" piece of balsa wood
✔ Matte medium gloss
✔ Narrow paintbrush
✔ Pencil
✔ Acrylic paint: blue, green, brown, red, white
✔ Hammer and nail
✔ 12" piece of thin wire

Step-by-Step Directions

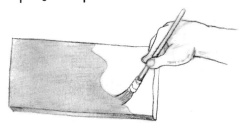

1. Paint the sky blue background on your balsa wood. Let dry.

2. Using pencil, sketch your design.

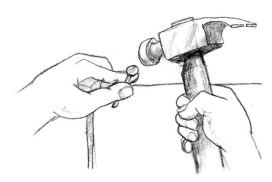

3. Color in your design detail with acrylic paint. Let dry.

4. Cover painted placard with gloss. Let dry.

5. To make holes in the top corners, hammer the nail into the wood and pull out.

6. Thread wire through the holes and twist wire closed.

> **BREEDOIDS: 1.** At two months old, **Pointers** have developed their hunting instinct, and can be seen crouching and stalking their prey. (In New York City, this tends to be pigeons!) **2.** The **Akita** has been one of Japan's official national treasures since 1931.

> **FACTOID:** Although to a human dog crates do not look like prime sleeping locales, dogs love them. It's their version of pure-cotton, 310-thread-count sheets and a cushy mattress pad over a Sealy posturepedic. Uh-oh, now it's nap time.

Kanine Key Hooks

f you are constantly misplacing your keys like I am, or you just drop your pup's leash on the top of a table somewhere like I do, you need to make yourself one of these key hooks that stars your own dog. I can't say I am a reformed key-and-leash slob, but at least having the option to hang up my keys and Scout's leash has helped me head in the right direction.

Difficulty Rating:

TOOLS & MATERIALS

✔ Sheet of tracing paper
✔ 2B pencil
✔ Picture of a dog
✔ Scrap of wood
✔ Acrylic paint: colors of your dog or dogs and background color
✔ Various-sized paintbrushes
✔ Hammer
✔ 2 saw-toothed picture hooks
✔ ¾" screw hooks
✔ Black permanent marker

Step-by-Step Directions

1. Using the pencil and tracing paper, trace the photograph or picture of a dog (or see Appendix B on page 149.)

2. Flip tracing paper over, place on top of the wood, and draw over the pencil marks that are now on the opposite side. This should leave faint pencil markings on the wood.

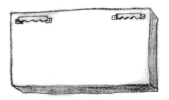

4. Turn wood over and hammer in 2 saw-toothed picture hangers, one in the top right-hand corner, and one in the top left-hand corner.

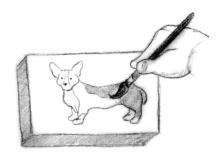

3. Paint the wood, both the background and the dog. Let dry.

5. Screw in the hooks on the front side under the image, leaving enough space between them to hang keys or a leash.

Two-Dog Key Hook

When you get a portrait done, it's not the size of the portrait that makes it hard, it's the number of bodies! True for the key hook craft as well. The German Shepherds on page 17 were easy to copy, but their shading was more demanding. I also wanted a little more detail so I added a topiary. If you really want to strut your stuff, paint two different positions of your pet, like the key hook with the Bull-

dogs. My husband and I are forever putting words into Scout's mouth. He'll look up at one of us and we feel the need to translate what is behind those little black eyes. Like I did with the Bulldogs and the Old English Sheepdog, you can add what your dog has to say using a black permanent marker.

Hints & Tips

- Reuse the tracing paper to make a mirror image of the dog, like on the German Shepherd hooks.
- If your dog is multicolored and you are not sure if you are up to the task of getting the various fur splotches correct, simply paint the dog's main colors.

- You can use 1 (versus 2) saw-toothed picture hanger, but it will be less stable when hung on the wall.
- Making a narrow hole with a drill first will help you screw in the hooks; however, a strong arm and wrist should get the job done, too!

BREEDOIDS: 1. Originally bred for the dangerous blood sport of bullbaiting, **Bulldogs** today may snort and breathe loudly, but it's usually because of their flat face, not because they think you're a bull. **2.** The **Pembroke Welsh Corgi** was brought to Britain in 1107 by Flemish weavers at the request of King Henry I. **3.** Rin Tin Tin, a **German Shepherd**, was the first canine movie star. In 1926 he starred in the silent film *The Night Cry*. He went on to star in five other films. **4.** The official Shaggy Dog, the **Old English Sheepdog**, is also called the Bobtail because of its docked tail.

FACTOID: When outside, the safest place for your dog is at the end of a leash.

Dogs-in-Art Tissue Box Cover

*F*or three years running, every February, to coincide with the dog lovers
flocking to the Westminster Kennel Club
Dog Show in New York, the William Doyle
Gallery pairs up with Bohnams & Brooks
of London to hold a dog (and sometimes
cat) sale. Dog lovers from all over come to
bid on dog art being auctioned off. Some
terrific sporting and nonsporting art ap-
pears at this event and single lots sometimes sell for over $100,000. This craft uses
some of the beautiful images of dogs in the
auction catalog.

Difficulty Rating:

TOOLS & MATERIALS

✔ Brown cardboard tissue box
✔ Acrylic paint: black and gold
✔ Small, narrow paintbrush
✔ 4 images of dogs in art
✔ 2B pencil
✔ Decoupage glaze
✔ Glue

Step-by-Step Directions

1. Paint the tissue box black. Let dry.

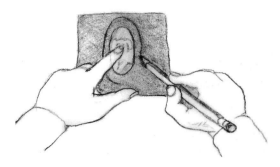

2. Trace the outline of the images on each side of the box. Draw another line around the pencil markings, making a frame for the image.

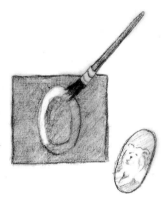

3. Place the images aside and paint each frame gold.

4. Once the gold frame is dry, attach images into their frames using glue. Then paint a layer of decoupage glaze over the entire box.

Dog Run Corkboard

For only dogs in New York, the dog runs scattered around the city are fun places to play. Scout particularly likes the small dog run at the Carl Schurz Park on the Upper East Side. He chases, sniffs, and mounts (much to his mother's distress) many other dogs.

This craft is a combination of decoupage and painting that allows for a lot of imagination. To give myself more space to decorate, I extended the wooden border of the corkboard by buying wider plywood

that I then nailed on. I used photos of dogs from magazines since the photos are much better than I could ever paint. However, I like painting my own hydrants, bones, chew toys, dog bowls, and dog beds. A layer of decoupage glaze protects the paper images and the paint.

Difficulty Rating:

TOOLS & MATERIALS

- ✔ Corkboard
- ✔ Ruler or yardstick
- ✔ 4 pieces of 2" wide and ¼" deep plywood that matches the length of your corkboard
- ✔ Hammer
- ✔ ¾" nails
- ✔ Acrylic paint: green, blue, white, yellow, red
- ✔ Various-width paintbrushes
- ✔ Dog images
- ✔ White glue
- ✔ Decoupage glaze

Step-by-Step Directions

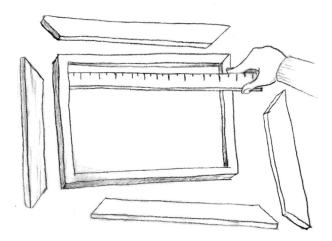

1. Measure the length of the corkboard's *inside* frame. Go to a lumber supply company and have them cut you four pieces of plywood to the dimensions you measure.

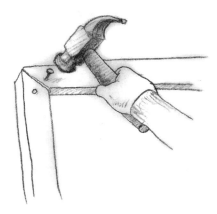

2. Nail plywood to the cork frame. This will give you more space to decorate.

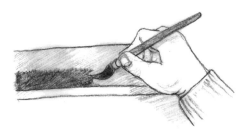

3. Paint the grass and sky on all sides of the frame. Let dry.

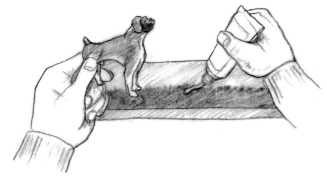

4. Glue on dog images.

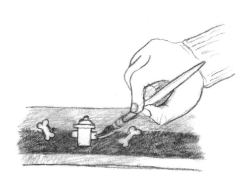

5. Paint bones, fire hydrants, squeaky toys, dog beds, and any touches you want to add, and let dry.

6. Coat the frame with decoupage glaze.

Hints & Tips

- Make sure the lumberyard cuts the ply-wood's dimensions for the inside length—not the outside. Otherwise you will shrink the size of usable space on the corkboard.

> **BREEDOID:** The **Boxer** is named because when it fights it strikes out with its front paws, making it resemble a human boxer.

Bone Bales

I found a reprinted paperback of an old Sears Roebuck & Co. catalog from 1902 and fell in love with it. I am a catalog fiend and shop more from catalogs than I do in stores. There's something so relaxing about coming home after a long day and sitting on the couch and rummaging through catalogs. All the items I could buy! I dog-ear pages and force myself to wait at least two days before ordering; immediate gratification means frequent trips to the post office later. When I brought home this 1902 catalog from the used bookstore, I practiced my normal routine. However, I'm able to go back in time with this catalog. I imagine dreaming of being able to afford a three-dollar stagecoach, or a four-dollar piano. I also wonder what sort of damage Dr. Rose's Arsenic Complexion Wafers caused its eager users, or how Dr. Worden's Female Pills for Weak Women solved all of our weaknesses.

Though 1902 was one hundred years ago, people loved their dogs. The catalog offers many items that celebrate dogs, like silver napkin rings with figures of dogs and rugs with the faces of Pugs. Today, by decoupaging photocopies of the ads, you can put these glorious ten-cent offerings on any object you choose and keep them alive for another hundred years or so.

Difficulty Rating:

TOOLS & MATERIALS

- ✔ Metal container
- ✔ Black acrylic spray paint
- ✔ Gold paint
- ✔ Small, narrow paintbrushes
- ✔ White glue
- ✔ Photocopies of old dog images
- ✔ Water-based acrylic urethane gloss

Step-by-Step Directions

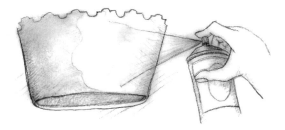

1. Spray paint the metal holder. Recoat until covered evenly and well. Let dry.

2. Using paintbrush and gold paint, paint gold edging.

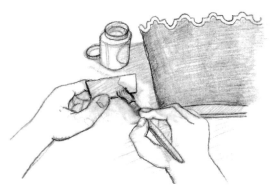

3. Using white glue, glue on dog images.

4. When dry, cover holder and images with the glaze.

FACTOID: One of today's best catalogs for dog lovers is *In the Company of Dogs*, which sells irresistible dog-inspired items. The catalog challenges owners everywhere to put it down *without* dog-earring most of its pages.

Stenciled Bone Bale

Y*ou can do a variety of things to these containers. Consider using the tracing outlines in Appendix B on page 149 to capture a different effect.*

P A R T

All Paws
on the Table

Tabletop Decorations

Featuring Fido and

His Friends

T W O

Lyin' Dog Place Card Holders

Who better to welcome your guests to their seats than a lyin' dog? Occasionally I wonder if some of my dinner guests wouldn't rather be lyin' down themselves. You can mold similar dog figures and paint them the same or different colors, or you can make the craft a little harder and make different breeds of dogs. Making any dog breed is possible; just be careful not to break off the tail!

Difficulty Rating:

TOOLS & MATERIALS

✔ Self-drying clay
✔ Moist sponge
✔ Bowl of water
✔ Clay tools or a butter knife
✔ Clay sealer
✔ Small, narrow paintbrush and fine-point paintbrush
✔ Acrylic paint: black, brown, white
✔ Matte-medium decoupage gloss

Step-by-Step Directions

1. Mold dog figure from clay. Use moist sponge if clay hardens while molding.

2. Using the knife, make a horizontal split in the dog's mug to make its mouth. Let dry.

3. Cover the clay figure with the clay sealer. Let dry.

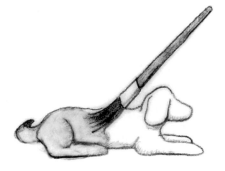

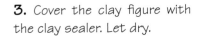

4. Using acrylic paint, paint the dog. Repeat until the dog's color is opaque. Let dry.

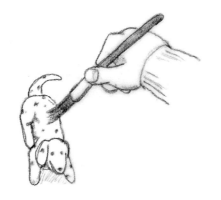

5. Using the matte-medium gloss, paint the dog for both protection and shine.

Hints & Tips

- Think of the figure of the dog in pieces to make it a more manageable project. (See the sidebar of the Tassel That Wags the Dog on page 10.)
- Water helps moisten dry clay and rid your figure of indentations and lines, but use it sparingly since too much water weakens the clay.
- When joining the pieces of clay together—for example, the hind leg to the body—make a tic-tac-toe pattern on each piece and moisten slightly. This will help the pieces adhere.

BREEDOIDS: 1. Dalmatians were much loved by Martha Washington, our country's first first lady. George Washington bought her a Dalmatian on August 23, 1787. **2. Labrador Retrievers** are the most popular dog in the United States, followed by **Golden Retrievers** and **German Shepherds.**

FACTOID: A dog tries to lick its owner's lips because as a puppy it got more food by finding a forgotten piece around its mother's mouth.

13

Mug-for-Me Decoupage Plates

Have you ever seen a picture of a dog in an advertisement that is so cute you want to go right out and buy one?

Well, if you make these plates, you can bring that very dog into your home without the added responsibility. Dogs have been used to sell products for years, and these days it is no different. Every time you come across an adorable mug in your favorite magazine, rip it out and keep him.

For this craft I like to photocopy the photo instead of using it straight out of the magazine. It allows for a little more creativity and it prevents the ad or text on the other side from bleeding through the image.

The head of the Bichon is almost an undoctored photocopy (since the real thing is white), unlike the Bulldog, which needed to be completely colored. A gold trim adds a nice touch, but the plates also look good without it. Consider the plate size versus the size of the dog's face or body before you start to glue.

Difficulty Rating:

TOOLS & MATERIALS

✔ Images of dogs
✔ Colored pencils
✔ Scissors
✔ Clear 7" or 9" plates
✔ White glue
✔ Foam "brush"
✔ Paint for glass: any color(s)

Step-by-Step Directions

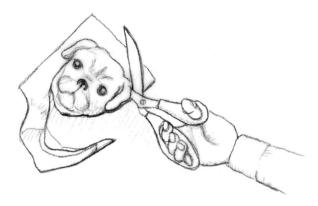

1. Photocopy the image of the dog, enlarging or shrinking as necessary for the size of your plate.

2. Using colored pencils, color the dog. Cut image out.

3. Hold the picture of the dog behind the glass plate with the image side against the glass, to consider where you want it to go.

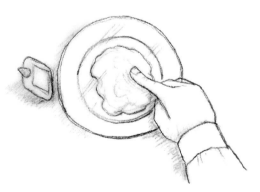

4. Using your finger or foam brush, put the white glue on the backside of the glass where the picture will eventually stick. (This is because colored pencils will sometimes "run" or smudge when wet. It is safer to put the glue on the plate versus putting the glue on the colored dog.) Make sure you cover all areas with glue that the picture will touch. (You can wipe away the excess glue easily, but if the picture is not completely glued down, the paint will seep under it and ruin the face. Let dry. Don't worry—it will dry clear!)

5. Stick the image, colored side on the glue, onto the plate.

6. Paint the edge gold and then once it is dry, paint the back of the plate completely, not only the glass but also the picture. Repeat as much as necessary (often three times). Make sure that the paint color is as opaque as possible when held up to the light.

Hints & Tips

- Mix a little bit of water with the white glue before gluing. When glued, the picture will have fewer air bubbles.

BREEDOIDS: 1. Of the four types of Swiss Mountain Dogs, the **Bernese Mountain Dog** is the most popular. However, the **Great Swiss Sennehund, or Swissy,** is gaining popularity in the United States. **2. Bichon Frise** means "stirred-up beard" in French, named after the dog's corkscrew tresses. **3.** An English slang dictionary from 1780 says that the definition of **Pug** is "something tenderly loved," proof that this dog already had a firm grasp on Britain's heart. **4.** In the nineteenth century the **English Bulldog** went to France, and gradually a **French Bulldog** was bred, some say with a slight influence of Terrier.

Give-a-Dog-a-Bone Place Mats

*T*his craft is terrific fun to make by your-self, or even better, with kids. When making this project with kids I suggest us-ing a water-soluble paint like tempura. However, if you use water-soluble paints (versus acrylic), make sure that when the place mats are complete, you coat them with a layer or two of water-based glaze, so spills, when they happen at mealtime, won't destroy all your hard work. Using acrylic or oil paint will make damage less likely, but it still doesn't hurt to protect your place mats from those of us who tend to drop our kibble all over the table.

Difficulty Rating:

TOOLS & MATERIALS

✔ 4 12" x 16" pieces of floor cloth
✔ Profile image of a dog
✔ 2B pencil
✔ Access to a photocopy machine
✔ Acrylic paint: black, white, red, blue, green, yellow
✔ Various-sized paintbrushes
✔ Scissors
✔ Water-based acrylic urethane glaze

BREEDOIDS: 1. Chihuahuas are the smallest breed of dog. Although they usually weigh between two and six pounds, their personality seems a lot bigger. **2. West Highland White Terriers,** commonly known as **West-ies,** as a breed, love to curl up in front of a fire. **3. Labrador Retriev-ers,** not from Labrador but from Newfoundland, are called St. John's Water Dogs in Newfoundland. **4. Dachshunds** are still used today to hunt wild boar in some countries.

Step-by-Step Directions

1. Using a pencil, either sketch the shape of a dog onto each piece of floor cloth (place mat) freehand, or enlarge an image of a dog on a photocopy machine, cut it out, and trace it. (See Appendix B on page 149 for the dog image.) Add a bone or bones to each place mat.

2. Paint your design. Let dry. Repaint if necessary.

3. Once the paint is dry and the mats are to your liking, paint or spray on a layer or two of water-based glaze.

Hints & Tips

- Try to buy preprimed floor cloth. In craft stores it often comes in 2' x 3' rolls, which can be cut in fourths to make these place mats. Usually there is a smooth side and a rough side to the floor cloth. Paint the smooth side.
- Place mats come in many sizes; don't feel that yours have to be exactly the same size or shape as those I've suggested.

FACTOID: Some Hindus believe that if you mistreat a dog you will return to earth as a dog.

Dog Phrase Napkin Rings

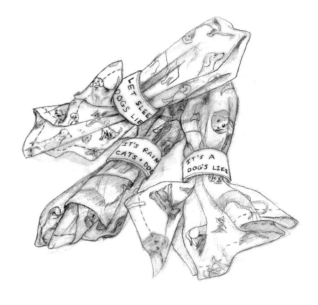

It's raining cats and dogs . . . It's a dog-eat-dog world . . . He's gone to the dogs . . . It's a dog's life . . . Let sleeping dogs lie. *Many dog phrases were born centuries ago, proof that man's best friend has held his place for many decades. There are dozens to choose from, some familiar, and some a little less so. Pick your favorites and adorn napkin rings with them. Choose one saying to use on all rings or a different saying for each one.*

Difficulty Rating:

TOOLS & MATERIALS

✔ 4–6 wooden napkin rings
✔ One color of acrylic spray paint
✔ Black permanent marker

Step-by-Step Directions

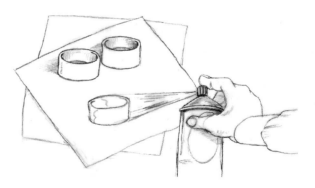

1. Spray paint the background of each napkin ring and let dry. Repeat if necessary.

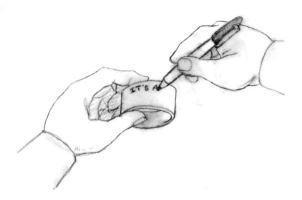

Hints & Tips

- Think about whether you want to write your slang once, twice, or three times on the ring before you start.

Dog Phrases

Every dog has its day
It's a dog's life
Let sleeping dogs lie
Gone to the dogs
It's a dog-eat-dog world
It's raining cats and dogs

2. Using the permanent marker, paint the dog phrase of your choice on each napkin ring. See suggestions here.

FACTOID: The saying *It's raining cats and dogs* is thought to have come from the Chinese since the spirit of rain was often depicted as a figure of a cat, and the spirit of wind was depicted as a figure of a dog.

BREEDOID: Alaskan Malamutes were used to pull sleds during the Klondike Gold Rush in Alaska in 1896.

16

No-Drool Napkins

I've written a children's book about the Saint Bernard, so I have a special place in my heart for this breed. When I thought of drooling dogs, St. Bs came right to mind. Even though cat lovers love to complain and make faces at dog lovers about our Drooling Dogs, isn't that part of the charm?

Like the bare-bones necessities listed below, you do not need much to do this craft. The prime-choice options will simply move the craft along a little faster, and they may provide a cleaner look (if you hand stitch the way I do). My husband and I hardly make it through a meal without getting food on our shirts. I fear we may be forgetting to chew (like our housemate, Scout). Fortunately, we both have no-drool napkins to tuck into our collars.

Difficulty Rating:

TOOLS & MATERIALS

Bare-Bones Necessities:
✔ 1 yard of dog fabric
✔ Ruler
✔ Scissors
✔ Pins
✔ Needle and thread

Prime-Choice Options:
✔ 1 yard of dog fabric
✔ Measuring tape
✔ Pinking shears
✔ Pins
✔ Iron
✔ Sewing machine

Step-by-Step Directions

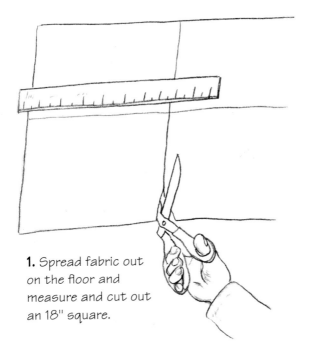

1. Spread fabric out on the floor and measure and cut out an 18" square.

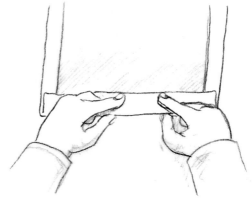

2. Fold over the edge of the square ½".

3. Fold it over ½" again.

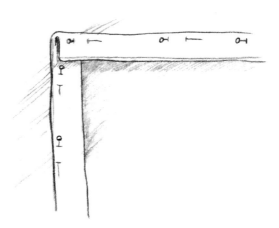

4. Pin folded edge down.

5. If possible, iron down the folded edges to make them flat.

6. Sew around the edge of the napkin.

Hints & Tips

- Along with the pins, ironing helps keep the rolled edges flat when you sew.
- You can make bigger napkins if you favor a larger size. Simply add a few inches to each side. The napkins described above will be 17" square.
- You can use scissors; however, pinking shears make the fabric's cut edge less apt to fray.

BREEDOID: Saint Bernards, who were used in the Swiss Alps to save snow-covered travelers, could find a person buried under seven feet of snow.

FACTOID: Humans have 5 million sensory cells for smelling in our nose. Dogs have between 100 and 240 million sensory cells. It is hard for us to even conceptualize how much more dogs are able to smell than we are.

17

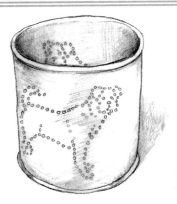

Lucky's Luminary

There is no doubt that Lucky is one of the most popular dog names for adopted dogs. Dogs that find homes are the lucky ones. One of Scout's best friends is named Lucky, and, as the best Luckys are, our Lucky is a midsized, shaggy bit of everything. I suppose there's a strand of Ti-betan Terrier in there (as his mom claims), but as far as we can see it's a small one. But we love Lucky even more because we don't know where he came from.

Luminaries are my favorite way to use candlelight. Whether they are hanging from a tree or are simple centerpieces on your dining-room table, the flickering light provides Halloween's jack-o'-lantern effect all year long. However, instead of the filtered light being in the shape of a star or heart, this craft brings Lucky to the table in luminary form (although if your Lucky's anything like Scout, the real-life version will already be there). An appropriate-sized image can be hammered into a one-of-a-kind luminary. If you want to, you can use the same image twice on each side of the can, or you can choose a second image, so you have two different images on the same luminary.

Difficulty Rating:

TOOLS & MATERIALS

✔ 2B pencil
✔ Tracing paper
✔ Image of a dog
✔ Masking tape

✔ Empty, smooth tin can
✔ Permanent marker
✔ 2 heavy books, a vice, or something to hold the can in place while hammering
✔ 25 pushpins
✔ Hammer
✔ Acrylic spray paint

Step-by-Step Directions

1. Using the pencil and tracing paper, trace an image of a dog that will fit on the side of the can. (See Appendix B on page 149 for an image you can use or enlarge.)

2. Cover the tin can with masking tape by wrapping it around the tin can.

3. Tape down the line-drawn image of the dog so that the pencil line is against the can. Retrace the image. This should leave a print of the image on the tin can.

4. Remove the tracing paper and go over the pencil image with a permanent marker.

5. Secure the can, and using the pushpins and hammer, punch holes in the can along the image. Keep the holes an equal distance apart.

6. When image is complete, remove masking tape.

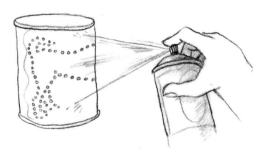

7. Paint the can with spray paint.

Hints & Tips

- Make sure that the tin can you use is smooth. The tin cans with rippled sides are tougher to hammer holes into and won't look as good.
- Even if you can draw the image on the can freehand, use the masking tape. It will help keep the pins from slipping when you hammer them in.
- To secure the can I sit on the floor with my back against a wall and hold the can between the soles of my feet! Although I look like a chimpanzee and my legs need a break every once in a while, it is the easiest, least expensive, and most reliable grip I have found.
- Expect to go through many pushpins. Either the plastic "handle" will chip off, making the pin tough to hold, or the metal part of the pin will bend.
- At first you may find it tough to make a hole with the pin and hammer. You might be tentative, fearing you'll hit your finger. However, the pin needs a good whack. A securely held can, a safe pinch of the tack with two fingers, and a hard, well-placed whack should give you a great hole.

BREEDOIDS: 1. Shar-Peis, a dog with roots in China, were once in danger of becoming extinct since the People's Republic of China taxed them so heavily that people could no longer afford to keep them. Fortunately, Shar-Peis were smuggled out and bred elsewhere. 2. The **Chow** is one of the oldest recognized breeds in the world and was once called the "black-mouthed dog," due to the dog's blue-black tongue.

FACTOIDS: 1. Not only was the ASPCA's founder, Henry Burgh, a champion of protecting animals, but he also led the crusade in the early 1870s to protect children from abusive parents. 2. Almost 25 percent of all dogs in shelters are purebreds.

Paw Print Magnets

This craft takes a steady hand, and it helps if you are patient. However, an impatient person can still make them. I'm proof. I made this craft glued to a television program about wild dogs in Africa.

Difficulty Rating:

TOOLS & MATERIALS

✔ Clear glass gems, round

✔ Pencil

✔ Colorful paper: wrapping, construction, wallpaper, etc.

✔ Scissors

✔ Black paper

✔ Tweezers

✔ Rubber cement

✔ ¾" round button magnets

✔ Strong clear household glue

Step-by-Step Directions

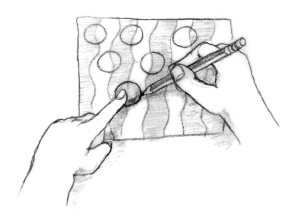

1. Using the pencil, trace the outline of the gem onto the back of the colorful paper, making a circle.

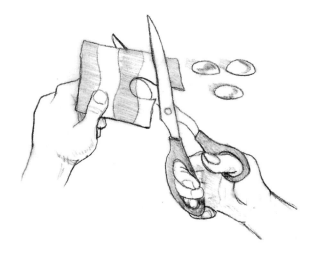

2. Cut out the circle from the colorful paper using scissors.

3. Cut out a dog's paw print from the black paper.

4. Using tweezers and rubber cement, glue the paw print to the colorful paper circle.

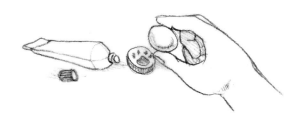

5. Glue the colorful paper circle to the magnet using the rubber cement.

6. Using the strong household glue, glue the clear gem to the magnet, on top of the paw print.

Hints & Tips

- Keep the magnets away from each other because they tend to attract. This can especially cause a problem at the gluing stage!
- Experiment with a few different paw prints before actually gluing the print to the paper. On my first try, my paw prints looked less like a dog's and more like a giant black bear's.
- The clear gem magnifies the paw, so make the paw a little smaller than you might be inclined to.
- Before gluing down the paper, make sure that it is not larger than the clear gem. If it is, you will be able to see the extra paper sticking out when looking at the magnet from the side.

FACTOID: Although the pads of a dog's paws have sweat-producing glands, they are not as sensitive to hot and cold as other areas of a dog's body.

BREEDOID: Shetland Sheepdogs, otherwise known as **Shelties,** are hunting dogs that originated in the Shetland Islands of Scotland.

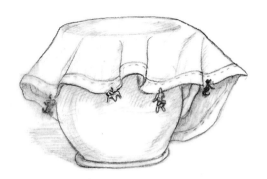

19

Poochie-Poo Pitcher Protector

*T*his craft helps keep the flies (and fleas) out of your pitcher of lemonade or iced tea during your spring and summer picnics and barbecues.

Below are the steps to make a lone pitcher cover, but consider making matching drink covers, too. Although I have suggested plain white fabric, substitute whatever crazy pattern you prefer. However, be sure that the fabric is light enough to be held down by the dog "weights." Most likely corduroy or velvet won't be held down by these light-weight dogs.

Difficulty Rating:

TOOLS & MATERIALS

✔ Measuring tape
✔ Fabric pencil
✔ ½ yard of white fabric
✔ Pinking shears
✔ Pins
✔ Needle
✔ White thread
✔ 8 hanging dog buttons or charms

Step-by-Step Directions

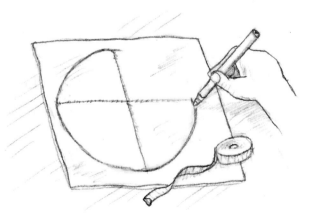

1. Using the measuring tape and fabric pencil, measure and draw a circle 16" in diameter on the fabric.

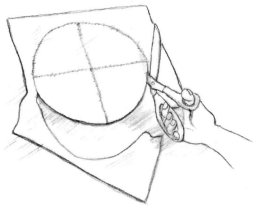

2. Cut out the circle.

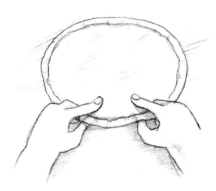

3. Fold over the edge ¼", twice. Pin into place.

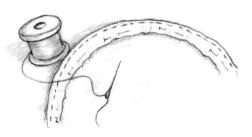

4. Using the needle and thread, sew the edge down.

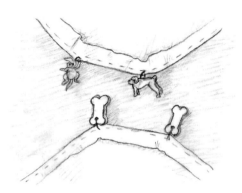

5. Sew the eight buttons or charms at an equal distance around the fabric.

Clay Bone Pitcher Protectors

Consider making the weights that hold the fabric down bone shaped and out of self-hardening clay. After molding the shape, make a hole in one end of the bone with a pencil tip or skewer, loop thread through the hole, and sew the thread to the fabric. Paint the bones white if you want to keep the color uniform, but consider painting them your favorite color or a variety of colors. You can make them ritzier by adding a touch of glitter, too.

Difficulty Rating:

20

Best-in-Show Lazy Susan

Every February, New York City rolls out the green carpet for the Westminster Kennel Club Dog Show, one of the pre-miere dog shows in the world. Hundreds of dogs come from around the country and the world to compete for the Best in Show. This year the slots for the twenty-five hundred contestants were filled within an hour of the entries opening. The two-day action happens in six rings simultane-ously, offering the viewer more to watch than possible. Madison Square Garden is buzzing with dogs and dog lovers. Beauti-ful dogs of all shapes, sizes, and personali-ties strut their stuff so well, you hardly notice the human handlers on the other end of their leashes. (Plus the event makes for some really good doggie shopping as well.) This craft incorporates the feel of a dog show by using the same color-copied image of different dog breeds. Each breed stars in its own ring, except this time you decide which one is Best in Show.

Difficulty Rating:

TOOLS & MATERIALS

✔ Fine sandpaper

✔ Wooden lazy Susan

✔ Acrylic paint: green, purple, yellow

✔ Water-based acrylic urethane gloss

✔ Various-sized paintbrushes

✔ 4 images of different dogs, each color copied 3 or 4 times

✔ Glue

Step-by-Step Directions

1. Using the sandpaper, lightly sand the lazy Susan.

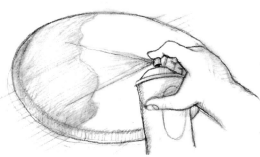

2. Coat with green paint, and repeat if necessary.

3. Once dry, using glue, paste images of the dogs around the edge of the lazy Susan.

4. Using the purple and yellow paint, paint the rings and Best-in-Show ribbon in the center of the circle. Let dry.

5. To protect it, cover the lazy Susan with water-based acrylic urethane gloss, as per directions on the can of gloss.

Hints & Tips

- Using green acrylic spray paint for the first round of painting will hasten the process.
- Use both big and small dogs, long haired and smooth coated.
- Dogs do not have to be facing the same way around the circle.
- Using a pencil, sketch the ring and Best-in-Show ribbon if you're not comfortable painting it right on.

FACTOIDS: 1. Two of the premiere dog shows in the world are the Westminster Kennel Club Dog Show, which began in New York in 1877 and has been held annually ever since, and the Crufts Dog Show, which began in London in 1886 and is also held annually. **2.** The USA Network provides coverage of the Westminster Kennel Club Dog Show every February, bringing the show into the homes of dog lovers everywhere. What a treat!

BREEDOIDS: 1. Weimaraners are gundogs who can both track and retrieve, unlike many dogs, who only retrieve. William Wegman, the renowned dog photographer, has brought a lot of deserved attention to the breed. In fact, every holiday season I can't seem to resist choosing his festive Weimaraner cards as the messengers of my holiday wishes. **2. Basset Hounds,** with their droopy ears and eyes, splayed toes, and loose skin, are thought to have Bloodhound ancestors. **3.** The **Cardigan Welsh Corgi** is believed to be the oldest British breed. The Celts brought the Corgi's ancestors to Wales around 1200 B.C. **4. Old English Sheepdogs** are gluttons for attention. Good training from puppyhood is the only way to keep these human lovers from jumping up.

PART

How Much
Is That Doggie in
the Window?

Picture Frames for

Your Furry Friend

THREE

Dog Tag
Picture Frame

I love my vet. Scout liked him, too, until he had that corncob he swallowed one Labor Day weekend surgically removed from his stomach. Since then Scout turns and tries to flee when we arrive at our doc's doorstep. Not me. My vet goes the extra mile and nowhere is that more clear than in this craft. He donated his outdated tags to my crafting cause. At his own risk. I keep these dog tags close to my chest because he informed me that people actually sell out-of-date dog tags to feign vaccination for their pet. You can ask your vet if he might consider donating his old ones to you, but watch out, because he's the one who gets in trouble if the tags fall into the wrong hands.

Although many of these tags are the same, you can vary the look by using different-shaped tags as well as tags made from different materials. Since green and gold go well together and Scout's dog tags are brass, I chose a hunter green background color. When you are planning your frame think about the color of the tags and pick the background color accordingly.

Difficulty Rating:

TOOLS & MATERIALS

✔ 5" x 7" wood picture frame
✔ Acrylic paint: green, black, gold
✔ Paintbrushes: 1 small and narrow, 1 fine-pointed
✔ 10 outdated metal dog tags
✔ Strong glue

Step-by-Step Directions

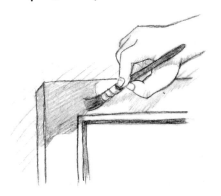

1. Paint the entire frame green.

2. Lay the dog tags on the frame where you would like them to go, and then glue them down one by one.

3. When dry, paint the inside rim of the frame gold. Let dry. Then paint a narrow black line around the gold line.

Hints & Tips

- Sanding the edges of the wood is a pain, but the final product looks better.
- Using acrylic spray paint hastens the painting process and also gives a streak-free look (as long as you don't overspray an area).
- If you are a fan of gold frames or don't want the gold tags to stand out so much, consider painting the whole frame gold before adding the gold tags.

BREEDOID: Beagles and their ancestors have been used as hunting dogs since the fourteenth century and were sometimes carried in the saddlebags of a riding hunter.

FACTOID: Fifty-five hundred dogs and cats are born in the United States every hour.

22

A Frame Good Enough to Eat

No doubt Fifi will look even more adorable surrounded by her favorite treats, whatever size or flavor they are. Just make sure this craft is out of her reach; otherwise you might catch her eating it. For various effects, try using different-colored frames and different-colored biscuits. A beige biscuit on a light wood frame will look different than multicolored biscuits on a black frame. You can also use lots of biscuits and place them end to end, or a few biscuits and place one on the top of the frame and one on the bottom.

Difficulty Rating:

TOOLS & MATERIALS

✔ Small, narrow paintbrush
✔ Clay sealer
✔ 8 to 12 small dog bone biscuits
✔ 5" x 7" or 4" x 6" picture frame
✔ Strong household glue

Step-by-Step Directions

1. Using paintbrush and clay sealer, paint the front and back of each dog biscuit and let dry.

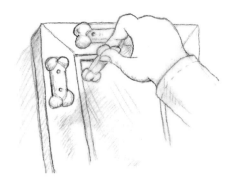

2. Lay dog biscuits on frame where you want them to go.

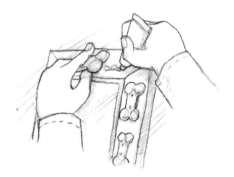

3. Using strong glue, lift each biscuit up, place a good squeeze of glue on the frame, and stick down. Continue around the frame.

Hints & Tips

- Even though the sealer will take away some of the smell of these treats, keep your frame away from your dog's nose. For example, if your dog is allowed up on the couch, don't place your frame on the side table.
- Make sure that the biscuits are all turned the same way around the frame. For example, if there is writing on the biscuit, face all biscuits toward the inside or outside of the frame.

BREEDOID: Originally owned by Chinese royalty, the **Shih Tzu** (under two layers of fur known as a "double coat") holds itself very proudly as it walks.

Pet Silhouette

I love colonial silhouettes, and one day when I have kids, I might make some of them, too. Until then I'll just make them of my dog and all the other pooches I love. I have one of Scout's cousins Charlotte, a Dachshund, and Becket, a black Standard Poodle infamous in the town of Port Washington, New York, for riding solo in the backseat of a taxi whenever a taxi driver finds him out wandering. I even made one of a Scottie (Scottish Terrier) just because I think they are cute.

STRIKING THE RIGHT POSE

Profile or head-on? Sitting, standing, or moving? Your number-one goal is to make your pet silhouette recognizable. For example, a pointer in profile standing up straight will not be as demonstrative (or look as good, in my opinion) as a pointer in profile with his nose outstretched, his front leg bent at an angle, and his tail pointed ruler-straight behind him. Also think about including more than one silhouette. The head-on Scottie silhouette, when added to the more traditional side-view silhouette, adds dimension to the piece. Think about the size of your dog, too. If you have a big dog, filling up the frame will give the viewer the idea that the dog is big, and vice versa for a small dog. A tiny silhouette of a Chihuahua will look adorable taking up only one-tenth of a frame.

Difficulty Rating:

TOOLS & MATERIALS

✔ Picture of a dog in profile

✔ Masking tape

✔ Tracing paper

✔ Sharp pencil

✔ Black paper

✔ Sharp scissors

✔ Double-sided tape

✔ White paper

✔ Picture frame

Step-by-Step Directions

1. Using masking tape, tape the tracing paper securely over the image you want to trace, and trace it. (See Appendix B on page 149.)

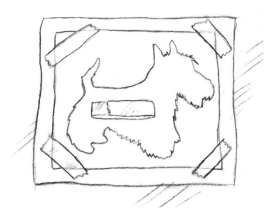

2. Once the image is traced, remove the tracing paper and tape it onto the black paper. Stick a piece of tape in the center of the traced animal so when the outer paper is cut off the image remains taped to the black paper.

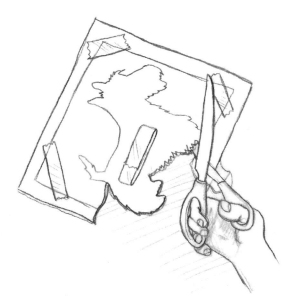

3. Carefully, using sharp scissors, cut out the image from the tracing and black paper.

4. Using double-sided tape, mount black image onto white paper and frame it.

THE HISTORY OF SILHOUETTES

Silhouettes are solid profiles—usually cut from black paper—of a person, an object, or, in our case, an animal. Silhouettes in varied forms have existed since the Stone Age, proof initially being found on cave walls. However, silhouettes became closer to their present form in the seventeenth century when a subject was backlit with a candle and the profile painted. It was not until the eighteenth century when paper became widely available that silhouettes as we know them were created.

The silhouette in its present form is named after a former French controller general of finance, Etienne de Silhouette, who lived from 1709 to 1767. In his spare time, Monsieur Silhouette cut people's profiles from black paper. The skill became a popular way to make money and quickly spread throughout Europe since the required tools were easy to carry. By 1839 silhouettes had crossed the Atlantic Ocean and arrived in America.

Though a master silhouette artist would balk at the use of tracing paper (and deny it is a real silhouette) since the art is all about the freehand cutting of an image, we nonmasters can still enjoy creating our own silhouettes even if we cheat.

Hints & Tips

- Use your breed's profile outline from the back of the book (see Appendix B on page 149) or try to find a picture in a dog breed handbook.
- Use the sharpest scissors possible. Master artists use 6¼" surgical scissors.
- Pick a thinner paper for the black paper since it is easier to cut, its fibers are less visible close up, and when placed on top of the white paper it stands off the paper less, showing no shadow.
- Remember that this craft is meant to remind the viewer of a historical silhouette, and if you put your silhouette in a polka-dotted rainbow frame you just might lose the effect.

BREEDOIDS: 1. Poodles, once trained to dance on hind legs in circus troupes, love to make people laugh even today. **2.** The **Scottish Terrier** was popularized in America in the first half of the twentieth century and can still be seen in advertisements, cartoons, and other doggie ephemera from that time more than any other breed of dog. **3.** Despite their short legs, **Dachshunds** are great runners.

Playing Pooches Frame

Above my desk, I have an etching of a boy sitting sideways in a kitchen chair looking down at two small dogs, one white and one black. The white dog is on his back, tummy exposed, and his front legs are sticking straight up in the air. His hind legs are slightly cocked just in case he needs to push the other dog off of him. The black dog is standing over the white dog, head askew, tongue hanging out of his mouth, eyes open wide, watching the white dog below him, one paw resting on the white dog's chest. The image is titled: Playmates.

What is more fun to watch than dogs at play?

This craft uses basic decoupage, but with an image of your own dogs playing. If you are like me you have hundreds of photos of your dog looking adorable: sitting, stretching, eating, sleeping, romping, and doing whatever she or he does the cutest. By taking that picture and color copying it, you can decoupage your own little wonder at play onto a frame. With acrylic paint and paintbrushes you can also add a few doggie touches such as balls and bones like I did.

Difficulty Rating:

TOOLS & MATERIALS

✔ Color copy image(s) of your dog
✔ Scissors
✔ 4" x 6" or 5" x 7" picture frame
✔ White glue or matte medium gloss
✔ Fine-pointed paintbrushes
✔ Acrylic paint: yellow, white
✔ Water-based acrylic urethane glaze

Step-by-Step Directions

1. After cutting out your images, lay them out on your frame. Then place glue on the backside, and glue them down.

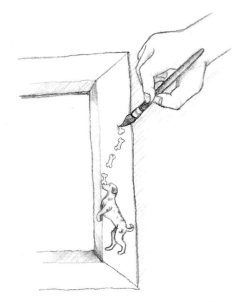

2. Using a paintbrush, paint tennis balls, bones, or other favorite toys.

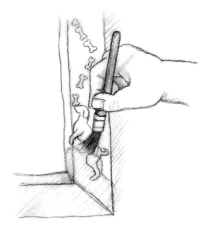

3. Once both the paint and the glue are dry, using a clean paintbrush and the glaze, cover the images. Let dry, and repeat as per directions on the back of the glaze.

Hints & Tips

- Don't glue on and paint glaze over your actual photograph. The glaze will ruin it. Be sure to use a color-copied image.

All-About-Dogs Decoupage Picture Frame

Dog tchotchkes . . . I can never get enough. There are dozens of doggie items in catalogs that I always want. My house is already filled with too much doggie-kitsch, however. Fortunately this craft lets me have it all. I cut out everything I want and decoupage it onto a frame. From sachets to signs, pillows to pins, bookends to Bulldogs, somehow *they all make it into my home.*

Difficulty Rating:

TOOLS & MATERIALS

✔ Scissors
✔ Collection of doggie images from all your favorite places
✔ 4" x 6" or 5" x 7" picture frame
✔ White glue or matte medium
✔ Small, narrow paintbrush
✔ Water-based acrylic urethane gloss

Step-by-Step Directions

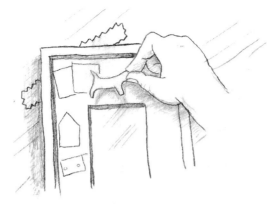

1. After cutting out all of your images, lay them out on your frame.

2. Pick each one up, place glue either on the frame or on the backside of the image, and glue down.

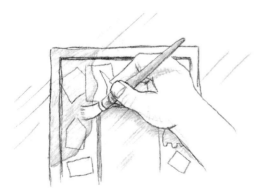

3. Once the glue is dry, using paintbrush and glaze, cover the images, and let dry. Repeat as per directions on the back of the glaze.

Hints & Tips

- You can paint your frame first if you don't like the colors they offer in the store.
- Consider gluing colored tissue paper down on the frame first, all over or just in some areas, before you glue on your images. This can add color and another dimension to the frame.

Get on
the Couch!

Pooch Pillows and
Other Stuffed Stuff

26-31

Pillow Talk: The Basics

Here's how to make your basic pillows and sachets. However, these directions assume that you don't want to remove what is inside the pillow. That is, if you want to wash the pillowcase, you'll have to wash it while it's on the pillow or you might ruin the inside of the pillow. Pillows with openings and decorative touches follow in Pugs & Pillows.

Step-by-Step Directions

1. Measure the fabric leaving enough room, about an inch or so, around all of the sides. This will allow for the stitches. If you would like to, use a fabric pencil to mark where you will cut. Measure again. (Once you cut, it's too late to remeasure if you mismeasured.)

2. Cut your fabric, preferably with pinking shears, into two pieces, a front and back panel.

3. Lay both pieces of fabric on top of each other, both right sides in, facing each other.

4. Pin the sides together, but leave an opening for the stuffing, another pillow, potpourri, etc.

5. Sew around all sides except for the hole, and turn the pillow right side out.

6. Fill the pillow. Sew the hole closed.

Note: Right vs. Wrong Side

When referring to the fabric, I use the term *right side* (e.g., right side facing up) and *wrong side* (e.g., wrong side facing in). The right side is the "front" side of the fabric or the side meant to be seen. The wrong side is the "back" of the fabric; it's often white or more muted in color. The reason I don't refer to the front side and back side of the fabric is that it becomes even more confusing when talking about the front side or back side of a craft! (For example, "Take the front side of the front side and lay it on the front side of the back side. . . ." See what I mean?)

Pugs & Pillows

Pugs have been at the feet of, in the arms of, and on the pillows of members of royalty for hundreds of years. Royal Pug owners include Josephine Bonaparte, Marie Antoinette, the Windsors, and Queen Victoria. However, royal figures are certainly not the only fans of these funny little creatures. My Aunt Diana, who, after falling in love with Max the Pug, has bought a lot of pretty adorable Pug paraphernalia, which now adorn her house.

In 2000, the Pug was the fifteenth most popular breed in America. Pugnus means "fist" in Latin, and it is probably because their scrunched-up little faces look like fists that they are so named. Despite these often odoriferous dogs' propensity for snoring, sneezing, and wheezing, this breed has such a faithful following that Pug owners often refuse to own any other breed.

Fabric companies today celebrate dogs in their latest patterns, and once again the Pug can be found taking top dog. This basic eighteen-inch pillow focuses wholly on the Pug mugs found on this colorful, cheery print. In this craft I take the basic pillow from Pillow Talk one step further: I add a fringe and a panel on the back of the pillow where you can stuff or unstuff your pillow.

Difficulty Rating:

TOOLS & MATERIALS

✔ 1 yard of Pug fabric
✔ Measuring tape
✔ Fabric pencil
✔ Pinking shears
✔ Needle
✔ Matching thread
✔ Pins

Step-by-Step Directions

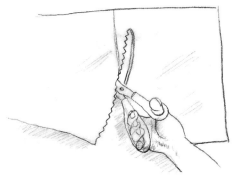

1. Measure a square 20" x 20" from the fabric, centering the Pugs. If you would like, use a fabric pencil to mark where you will cut. (This will be the front of your pillow.) Check your measurement again. Cut your fabric, preferably with pinking shears.

2. Measure and cut another piece of fabric 20" tall by 25" wide. Cut it in half so you have two pieces of 20" x 12.5" fabric. (These will be your back panels where you will slide in your pillow.)

3. Using remaining fabric, cut strips of fabric 5" wide. Connect the strips by sewing the ends together.

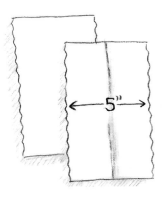

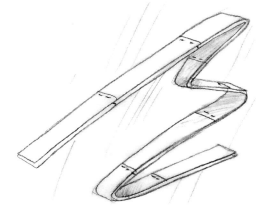

4. Make one long strip at least 88" long. (It doesn't matter how long the strips are as long as they become 88" long when they are sewn together.) Fold the long strip in half lengthwise, right side out, and pin the two sides together. (When bunched together, this will make your fringe.)

5. Take the two back panels. The two will overlap in the center of the pillow, so fold the center edges back, right side visible, and sew down. This allows you to "finish" the visible edges.

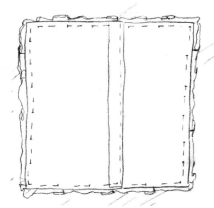

6. Now it's time to put it all together. Lay the front panel down, right side facing up. Place the fringe, the frilly part facing toward the center of the pillow and cut edge against the edge of the panel, along the edge of the front panel. Lay the back two panels on the front panels, right side facing down, so they match up, overlapping in the center of the pillow. Take out the pins you used for the fringe and pin the three pieces together, bunching up the fringe along the way so that when the pillow is right side out, the fringe will not be flat but wavy or frilly around the pillow.

7. Sew around the pillow, remove pins, and turn right side out.

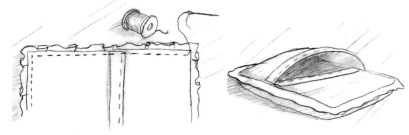

FACTOID: In the Middle Ages, people used dogs as foot warmers in church by having them lay on their feet.

Hints & Tips

- A sewing machine makes this go a lot faster.

Quote

"The uglier the dog, the more he or she is loved."—Martyn Lewis

Royal Pug Pillows

Royalty is for the birds unless, of course, you are royalty. So why not become royal? In fact, some members of my own family already act like royalty, so why don't we join them? These posh pillows will certainly make you feel like royalty if you missed out on that birth lottery.

Difficulty Rating:

TOOLS & MATERIALS

✔ 1 yard of green velvet fabric
✔ Measuring tape
✔ Fabric pencil
✔ Pinking shears
✔ 1 yard of Pug fabric
✔ Pins
✔ Needle
✔ Matching thread
✔ 1 yard of matching trim

Step-by-Step Directions

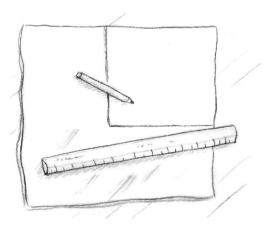

1. Measure one 20" square from the green velvet fabric. If you want to, use a fabric pencil to mark where you will cut. (This will be the front of your pillow.) Cut your fabric with the pinking shears.

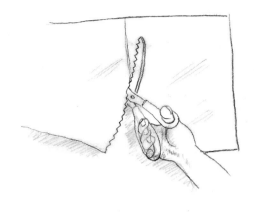

2. Measure and cut another piece of green velvet fabric 20" tall by 25" wide. Cut it in half so that you have two pieces of 20" x 12.5" fabric. (These will be your back panels where you will slide in your pillow.)

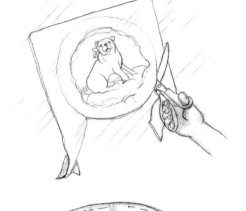

3. Cut out a 16" circle of Pug fabric, centered on the Pug's mug. Fold over ¼" of the fabric edge, with the right side folded over, and pin.

4. Take the two green velvet panels and, along one of each of the panels' 20" sides (where the two will overlap), fold back a ¼" edge, right side folded over, and stitch down.

5. Lay the 20" green velvet square down, right side facing up. Place Pug circle in the center. To make the fringe, wrap the trim around and under the Pug fabric, allowing the nice part to show. Take the pins out of the Pug fabric and incorporate them to hold down the Pug fabric, the trim, and the green velvet square (in that order).

6. Sew the Pug fabric, the trim, and the green velvet square together.

7. On top of the Pug square, lay the back two panels, right side facing down, so that they match up, overlapping in the center of the pillow.

8. Pin the green velvet panels to the Pug square and sew together.

9. Remove pins and turn right side out.

Hints & Tips

- A sewing machine makes this go a lot faster.

BREEDOID: The **Brussels Griffon** became much more popular after Queen Astrid of Belgium fell in love with her country's native breed. The dog's short nose makes it similar in appearance to the **Pug**.

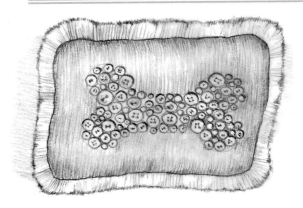

Hugo's Dog-Bone Button Pillow

I always miss Scout when I go away for vacation. Although the Bahamas wouldn't mind if I took Scout with me when I went to visit my grandmother, she probably would, so I don't impose. It makes for a tough toss-up. A vacation in the Bahamas? Or leave Scout at home? Poor Scout, the Bahamas always win. However, when I'm there I do miss him. Fortunately, there's Hugo. Hugo lives next door to my grandmother. Hugo was adopted and his parents think he's a roundabout Lhasa Apso. Hugo's parents are also kind enough to let me try to play with him. My ears prick up whenever I hear their front door open and Hugo's dog tags jingle. Hugo's going for a walk! I whirl out of my grandmother's front door like Wonder Woman and place my body and magic wristbands between Hugo and the steps that will take him to the rest room. Hugo's a little blasé about me, but that's okay, I forgive him. I still coo over him and pat him. I hope maybe he'll like me more if I name this pillow after him.

Difficulty Rating:

TOOLS & MATERIALS

✔ Measuring tape
✔ Pinking shears
✔ 1 yard of solid blue, textured fabric
✔ White fabric pencil
✔ A collection of white and ivory buttons, various sizes and shapes
✔ Needle
✔ White thread
✔ Blue thread
✔ 2 yards of fringe
✔ Pins

Step-by-Step Directions

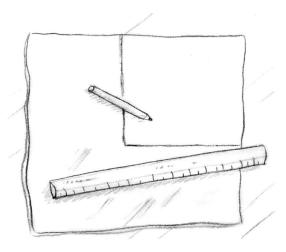

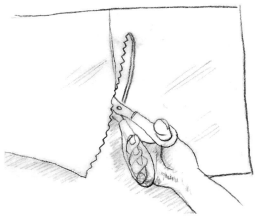

1. Measure and cut one 14" x 18" piece of fabric.

2. Measure and cut two panels of fabric 14" x 11" (these will overlap in the back and cover where you put in the pillow).

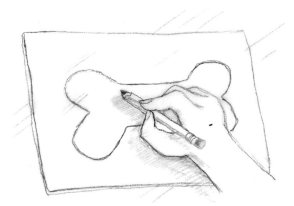

3. Using the white fabric pencil, sketch an image of a bone on the 14" x 18" piece of fabric, leaving at least 4" between the edge of the bone and the edge of the fabric on all sides.

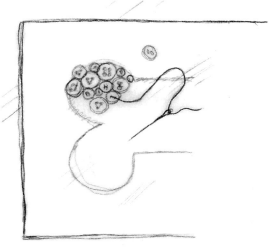

4. Fill in the bone shape by sewing on all of your buttons with white thread.

5. To make the back of the pillow, on each 14" x 11" panel of fabric, sew down a ¼" edge on one of the 11" sides.

6. Lay the fabric with the buttons faceup on the floor. Lay fringe around the edge so that the fluffy part of the fringe is facing toward the bone, or the center of the right side, and the unfrilly side of the trim is flush with the edge of the fabric. Lay the two 14" x 11" panels facedown on top of the fringe and bone so that sewn edges overlap in the center.

front panel   fringe   back panel

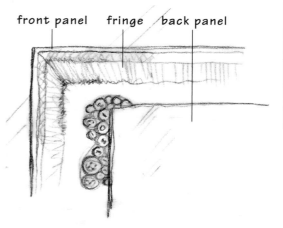

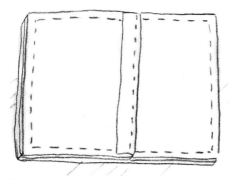

7. Pin together.

8. Sew around the edge, remove pins, and turn right side out.

Hints & Tips

- A sewing machine will allow you to do this project much more quickly.
- Try not to put the same buttons right next to each other.
- Don't worry if the buttons are not right against one another. When the craft is complete, the space between the buttons won't be noticeable.
- I used blue fabric because the white and ivory buttons stand out so well. You can use any color fabric. However, I recommend a solid, not a pattern, unless the pattern is very small.

FACTOIDS: 1. The word *dog*, depending on who is using it and when, can mean: in verb form, "to dress with care," "to treat someone badly," and "to engage in sexual intercourse"; and in noun form, "a low-ranking person," "a friend," and "a general male nickname." **2.** One female dog and her offspring can produce sixty-seven thousand dogs in five years.

BREEDOIDS: 1. Lhasa Apsos, whose origin belongs in Tibet, are good barkers. In fact, their name means "hairy barking dog." **2. Pekingese** are loyal to their masters, and they were bred to have bowed legs to keep them from traveling too far too fast.

My Baby's Name in Bones

I named Scout after Scout in the book To Kill a Mockingbird *by Harper Lee, not because Bichons are particularly skilled* scouters. *Although I had wanted a girl Scout, all the breeder had left was a boy Scout, so there it is. However original I thought his name was at the time (remember I also chose the name Fluffy for my childhood dog), today I realize there are Scouts all over the place. In fact, there's a miniature Dachshund named Scout who lives across the street from us. How is it possible that another dog who is not a Bichon and who is not my Scout is named Scout? And why am I territorial about his name? I wonder if my parents felt the same way after they named me Jennifer at the start of the seventies (clearly I inherited their keen ability to choose names). Despite having to share his name, in my household it is often all about Scout, and nowhere is it more clear than in this craft.*

Difficulty Rating:

TOOLS & MATERIALS

✔ A collection of dog bone buttons, in many sizes
✔ Ready-made baby pillow
✔ Painter's tape (often blue)
✔ Needle
✔ Thread the color of the bones

Step-by-Step Directions

1. Spell your dog's name in bones by laying bones on the pillow.

2. Using painter's tape, tear small, thin pieces and tape down the ends of the bones without covering the buttonholes.

3. Sew on each button.

4. Continue until all your bone buttons are sewn on. Take off the tape.

Hints & Tips

- You can make your own baby pillow, but a store-bought one works just as well.
- Make sure you have bone buttons in a variety of sizes. Or simply buy many small ones. Also, keep the length of your dog's name in mind, and therefore the size of the buttons, when buying them.

Scottie Pillowcase

Dog pillows are all over the place these days, and they are multiplying like an unneutered pup. I have always loved needlepoint dog pillows; however, I must admit the two currently adorning my couch are store-bought. The basic material cost to make one is so much more than the cost of the ready-made variety available in catalogs, I can justify buying them.

However, this doggie pillow is easy and inexpensive to make. You can even make it out of fabric scraps you have lying around if you are a packrat and save every little thing for possible future use like I do. The background fabric can be almost any color and pattern since the dog is large and solid black, and it makes enough of a statement to outweigh a busy and colorful background fabric pattern. However, as a matter of course, I recommend a Scottish plaid.

Difficulty Rating:

TOOLS & MATERIALS

✔ Measuring tape
✔ 1 yard of checked fabric
✔ Pinking shears
✔ Needle
✔ Thread that matches fabric
✔ Pins

✔ Access to a photocopier
✔ Image of a Scottie
✔ Scissors
✔ ¼ yard of black felt
✔ Small piece of pink felt
✔ Black thread
✔ 3 black buttons

Step-by-Step Directions

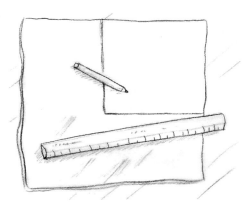

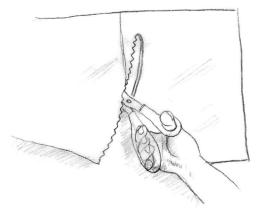

1. Measure a 20" square from the fabric. Cut your fabric, preferably with pinking shears.

2. Measure and cut another piece of fabric 20" tall by 25" wide. Cut it in half so you have two pieces of 20" x 12.5" fabric. (These will be your back panels where you will slide in your pillow.)

3. Using remaining fabric, cut strips of fabric, 5" wide.

4. Connect the strips by sewing the ends together. Make one long strip at least 88" long. (It doesn't matter how long the strips are as long as they are 88" long when they are sewn together.)

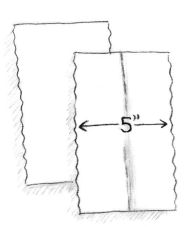

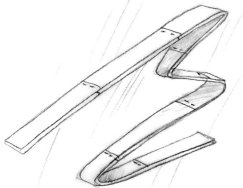

5. Fold the long strip in half lengthwise, right side out, and pin together. (When bunched together, this will make your fringe.)

6. Take the two back panels and, in the center where the two will overlap, fold the center back edges ¼", right side out, and stitch down.

7. Photocopy the image of a Scottie (see Appendix B on page 149), enlarging to desired size. With regular scissors, cut out image, pin to black felt, and cut out Scottie image from the felt. Put paper image of Scottie aside. From the pink felt, cut a tongue. Sew felt Scottie to the 20" square with the black thread, and sew on tongue and buttons for nose and eyes.

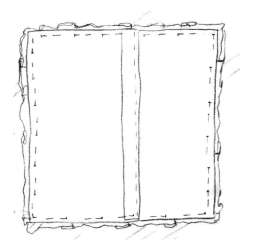

8. Lay down the front panel with the Scottie right side facing up. Place the frilly side of the fringe toward the center of the pillow and unfinished edge flush with the edge of the front panel. Lay the back two panels on the front panel, right side facing down, so they match up, overlapping in the center of the pillow. Take out the pins you used for the fringe and pin the three pieces together, bunching up the fringe along the way as you pin.

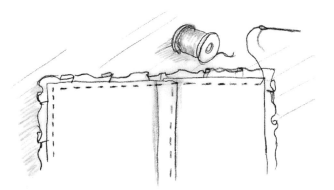 

9. Sew around the pillow. Take out pins.

10. Turn right side out.

BREEDOID: Scottish Terriers were originally bred to go underground to find small, pesky animals.

FACTOID: One of the most famous **Scotties** was Fala, FDR's first dog, who lived in the White House with him from 1942 to 1945.

Your-Dog-Here Pillow

*E*nough about other *dogs. I want a pillow with my dog on it!"* Since felt is such an easy fabric to work with, even multicolored canines can be featured on a fancy living-room couch pillow. All you need is the right color felt (or close to) and a needle and thread. Since felt won't fray like other fabrics, all you have to do is line up the edges and sew them to the background fabric. Easy enough. Below is a Maltese pillow that shows you can get really creative if you want: To better illustrate one of the Maltese's well-known qualities of long, luxurious white fur, I attached white ribbons to the figure. Like the real thing, this dog pillow's tresses blow in the wind. Even if your pooch isn't a Maltese, follow these directions to make a pillow starring your dog.

Difficulty Rating:

TOOLS & MATERIALS

✔ Measuring tape
✔ 1 yard of background fabric
✔ Pinking shears
✔ Needle
✔ Background-colored thread
✔ Pins

✔ Access to a photocopier
✔ Image of your dog (front-on, profile, standing, etc.)
✔ Scissors
✔ ¼ yard of felt in your dog's color
✔ Small piece of pink felt
✔ Dog-colored thread
✔ 3 buttons for nose and eyes
✔ 2 yards or so of grosgrain ribbon, if necessary

Step-by-Step Directions

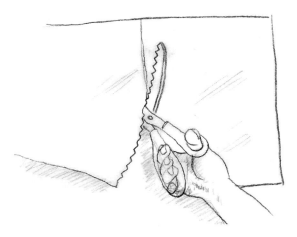

1. Measure a 20" square from the fabric. Cut your fabric, preferably with pinking shears.

2. Measure and cut another piece of fabric 20" tall by 25" wide. Cut it in half so you have two pieces of 20" x 12.5" fabric. (These will be your back panels where you will slide in your pillow.)

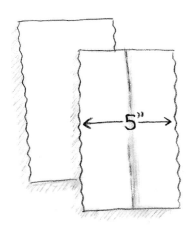

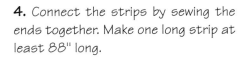

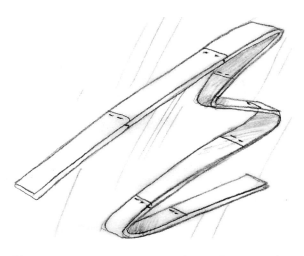

3. Using remaining fabric, cut strips of fabric, 5" wide.

4. Connect the strips by sewing the ends together. Make one long strip at least 88" long.

5. Fold the long strip in half lengthwise, right side out, and pin together. (When bunched together, this will make your fringe.)

6. Take the two back panels and, in the center where the two will overlap, fold the center edges back ¼", right side out, and stitch down.

7. Photocopy the image of your dog (see Appendix B on page 149), enlarging to desired size. Cut out the image with regular scissors, pin to the dog-colored felt, and cut out your dog's image in the felt. From the pink felt, cut a tongue with regular scissors. Sew your dog to the 20" square with the dog-colored thread, and then sew on the tongue and buttons. Sew on the grosgrain ribbon.

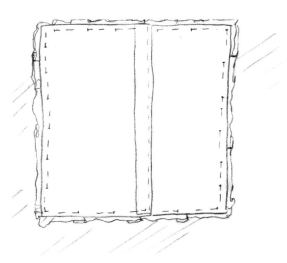

8. Lay down the front panel with your dog, right side facing up. Place the fringe, right side facing inward toward the center of the pillow, along the edge of the front panel, bunching and pinning as you go. Lay the back two panels on top of the front panel, right side facing down, so they match up, overlapping in the center of the pillow. Take out the pins you used for the fringe and pin the three pieces together, bunching up the fringe along the way.

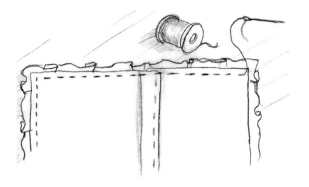 

9. Sew around the pillow. Take out pins.

10. Turn the pillow right side out.

BREEDOID: The **Maltese,** from the old island of Malta, is one of the oldest breeds of dogs. Charles Darwin believed that its origins date to 600 B.C. Throughout the breed's life it has been called a Maltese Lion Dog, Maltese Terrier, Ye Ancient Dogge of Malta, the Shock Dog (because of its hair), Melitaie (the ancient name for Malta) Dog, the Roman's Ladies' Dog, the Spanish Gentle, and the Comforter.

32 - 34

Doggie Sachets

Just as dogs have a distinct love for dirty laundry, most of their human friends like a clean, fresh smell. Sachets are little packets of fresh and clean that can find a place in any home. Sachets are terrific gifts and they are easy to make. Two of the sachets below are made just like the simple pillow in Pillow Talk: The Basics on page 71. The crafts below offer a variety of styles, although the tools that you need to make them are almost all the same.

The first sachet is the bundle sachet and is arguably the easiest. The second sachet shows off the dog-patterned fabric you choose, and the third focuses on a specific dog breed within the fabric. There are countless adorable dog-themed fabrics that celebrate both specific and varied dog breeds.

TOOLS & MATERIALS FOR ALL THREE SACHET PROJECTS

✔ 1 yard of dog fabric
✔ Fabric pencil
✔ Measuring tape
✔ Pinking shears
✔ Pins
✔ Needle
✔ Matching thread
✔ Dried lavender or other potpourri
✔ Matching ribbon
✔ Funnel

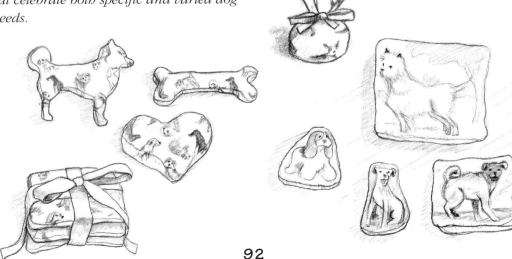

32. Bundle Sachet

Difficulty Rating:

Step-by-Step Directions for the Bundle Sachet

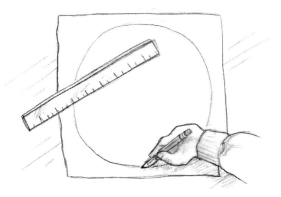

1. Lay out your dog-themed fabric, right side down, and draw a 16" circle.

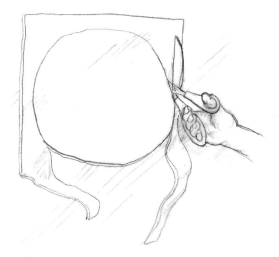

2. Cut out the circle with the pinking shears.

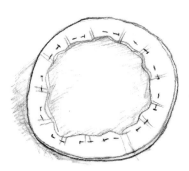

3. Fold back the outer 4" toward the center of the circle and pin.

 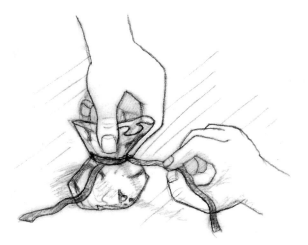

4. Sew down the folded fabric and place a clump of lavender in the center of the circle. Remove the pins.

5. Pull up the sides and tie them together with a tight knot and then a bow.

BREEDOID: Huskies have been used to herd reindeer and pull sleds for over three thousand years by the Inuit people of Alaska.

33. Shaped Sachet

Difficulty Rating:

Step-by-Step Directions for a Shaped Sachet

1. Fold your fabric in half, right sides facing each other, and choose the figure that you would like to create. Sketch the image onto the fabric.

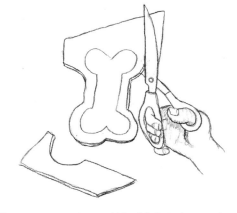

2. Leaving at least ½" of fabric beyond your sketch, cut out your shape, following the outline of the image.

3. Using needle and thread, sew around the fabric on the sketch mark, leaving at least a 1" hole for the pot-pourri filler.

4. Turn sachet right side out and fill with lavender, using the funnel.

5. Sew the 1" hole closed.

34. Single Breed Sachet

Difficulty Rating:

Step-by-Step Directions for a Single Breed Sachet

Some fabrics use a specific dog breed and it's fun to make sachets that star that breed. Try using a second fabric for the back of the sachet.

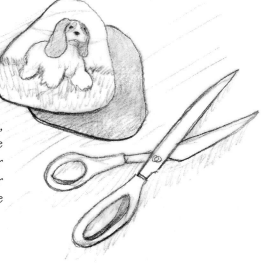

1. Cut from the fabric the image of the dog, leaving at least ¼" around it to sew. With the right side in, cut a matching shape from either the same fabric or another piece of fabric—for example, a plain fabric that shares the same background color.

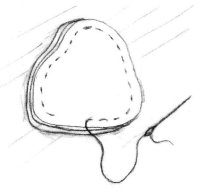

2. Place the fabric together, right side in. Sew ¼" or so from the edge of the fabric, leaving a 1" hole somewhere along the edge for the filler.

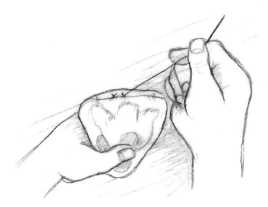

3. Turn right side out and fill with lavender, using the funnel.

4. Sew the hole closed and add ribbon.

Hints & Tips for Sachets

- A sewing machine can make these sachets a lot easier and go a lot faster.
- You can use scissors if you do not have pinking shears; however, pinking shears are preferable, since they make the fabric less apt to fray.
- A chopstick is a terrific help when turning your sewn sachet inside out. Either the thick or thin end of the chopstick can be placed through the hole and pushed and maneuvered for hard-to-reach places.
- You can make a funnel out of plain white paper by rolling it, sticking one end into the pocket of the sachet, and pouring the lavender or potpourri into the wider end.

- If you don't have a fabric marker, an artist's pencil also works.
- Consider using a plain fabric for the back side of the sachets in the second and third projects. This will save you money since plain fabric is often less expensive than dog fabric.
- Do not forget to leave a hole when you are sewing! The hole should be large enough for your finger to fit through with a little extra space. When in doubt, make the hole bigger rather than smaller.
- If your sachet is going to be large and you do not want to use a lot of lavender, place batting or polyester fill into the sachet to bulk it up, and then add the scent.

Antique Dog-Button Pillow

I have always been a collector, and of late, my collecting has consisted of all things dog. If you have a love of buttons, this is your craft. Over time I have collected numerous dog buttons that vary in appearance, price, and availability. From brightly colored plastic buttons from America made in the 1940s, to pewter buttons signed and dated by the artist; from hand-sculpted ceramic buttons from South America, to special-order brass hunting buttons from France; from miniature carved mother-of-pearl puppies, to enameled Scotties—all these buttons focus on one thing: dogs. I bought some of these buttons for a few cents and others for many dollars; some were purchased from specialty stores, some off the Web, and some by the bag in nationwide megacraft stores. Although in my collection I chose to focus on dogs only (and not their bones, dishes, hydrants, and leashes), many dog-related buttons are out there, too. I chose a pillow antique in feeling because some of the buttons themselves are pretty old.

Difficulty Rating:

TOOLS & MATERIALS

✔ Needle
✔ White thread
✔ Collection of dog buttons
✔ Baby pillow

Step-by-Step Directions

1. Thread needle.

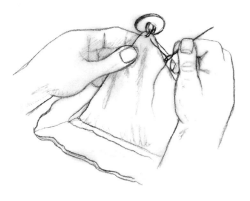

2. Sew on a button.

3. Continue until all your favorite buttons are sewn on.

Hints & Tips

- You can make your pillow, but a store-bought one like I used for this craft works just as well.
- Consider the placement of the buttons before you sew them on. If you have many round buttons, don't place them all in the same area; break them up a bit. Likewise, if you have similar-looking buttons with only a slightly different scene or color, separate them.

BREEDOID: The **Great Dane** was bred initially to hunt wild boars. The name is thought to have come from the old French designation *grand Danois*, which means "big Danish."

FACTOID: Hunting dogs and **Greyhounds** are found on many of the earliest buttons and seals that feature dogs.

Quote

"Dog lives are too short. Their only fault, really."—Agnes Sligh Turnbull

Paper Training
for Humans

Woofer Wrappings
and Supplies

Sammy Stamps

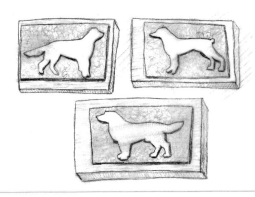

*S*am, or a derivation thereof, is one of the most popular dog names, and it is certainly true in my life so far. In my immediate family we have had two Sams, a Samantha, and a Sammy. They were all mutts; in only one case did we have the faintest idea from who or what she came. Despite (or because of) their mutt status, all four were superb pets, especially those who had previously been abused. I named this craft after our Sammys because each one deserves it.

Difficulty Rating:

TOOLS & MATERIALS

✔ 2B pencil
✔ Tracing paper
✔ Dog images
✔ Sheet of flexible foam
✔ Scissors
✔ Thin, flat piece of corkboard
✔ X-Acto knife
✔ Flat piece of balsa wood, ¼"
   thick
✔ Rubber cement
✔ 2 heavy books

Step-by-Step Directions

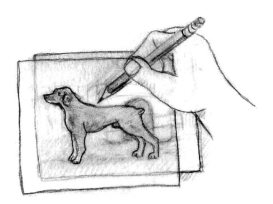

1. Using a pencil and piece of tracing paper, trace the image you want to make into a stamp (see Appendix B on page 149).

2. Lay the image onto the sheet of foam, and trace it.

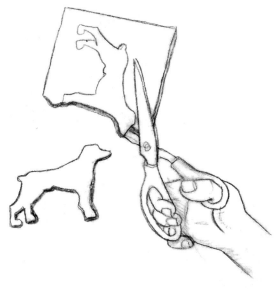

3. Cut it out and repeat Step 2 so that you have two identical (or almost identical) foam images.

4. Lay one of the foam images onto the piece of cork and cut out a slightly larger piece of cork with the X-Acto knife that will encompass the image. Lay the cork onto the balsa wood, and, with the X-Acto knife, cut balsa wood even larger than the cork shape.

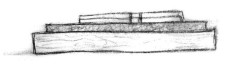

5. Using rubber cement, place glue between the two pieces of foam and stick together.

6. Then glue the foam to the cork, and then the cork to the wood.

Hints & Tips

- When gluing, you can separate each step in Steps 5 and 6. For example, I put glue on each side of the foam image of the dog, stuck it together, and then placed it under a book to dry. Ten minutes later, I uncovered the foam dog, put glue on one side of the image, put glue on the cork, and placed it back under the book to be sure it all dried flat and evenly. I repeated the steps to glue the cork to the balsa wood. However you choose to glue the pieces together, just be sure that when the stamp pad is finished, it is completely flat so that the stamp works.
- Do not use too much glue. Just place a clean, even layer onto the entire form.
- Use glue on both of the sides that will be glued together. This helps make the bond stronger.

BREEDOIDS: 1. The **Doberman Pinscher** was created in the 1870s by Louis Doberman, a German tax collector, by combining a **Weimaraner,** a **Rottweiler,** a **German Pinscher,** a **Greyhound,** and a **Manchester Terrier. 2.** The **Golden Retriever,** one of the most popular family breeds, was once used to retrieve fowl from the water. **3.** The **Irish Setter,** a product of Ireland, was once called Madradh Ruadh, which means "red dog."

FACTOID: The ASPCA was founded in 1866, a year after the thirteenth amendment was passed to abolish human cruelty and enslavement.

37

Bone and Hydrant Sponge Stamps

*C*rafts don't get much easier than this. However, depending on the size of your stamp and your own creative juices, you can use the stamps to make all kinds of cards, wrapping paper, and decorative boxes or packages. You can even "stencil" furniture. Even a novice crafter can make and use this craft.

Difficulty Rating:

TOOLS & MATERIALS

✔ 2 kitchen sponges
✔ Ballpoint pen
✔ Scissors

Step-by-Step Directions

1. Wet the sponges and squeeze out all the excess water.

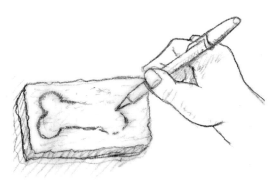

2. Using the ballpoint pen, draw the shape of a hydrant on one sponge and a bone on the other.

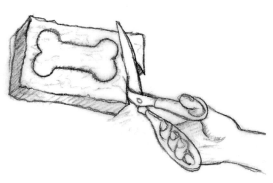

3. Cut out the images.

Hints & Tips

- It's much harder to cut the sponge dry.
- Use sharp scissors.

BREEDOIDS: 1. The **Norfolk** and **Norwich Terriers** are almost exactly alike except for their ears. The Norfolk's ears fold over, and the Norwich's stand erect. **2.** The **Jack Russell Terrier** was named after John Russell, an English Reverend who bred very successful fox dogs in the nineteenth century.

FACTOID: There are twenty-nine breeds of terrier today, and as a group, they have won more than any other at the Westminster Kennel Club Dog Show.

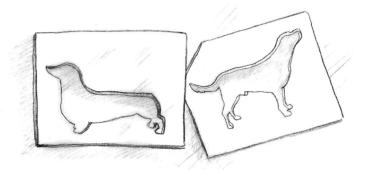

38

Who Let the Dogs Out? Stencils

*C*raft stores sell plain sheets of plastic for people who want to make their own stencils. All you need are images of dogs, and scissors or an X-Acto knife. Once you have made your stencils, your crafting possibilities are endless. Stencil the image on walls, bureaus, paper, envelopes, boxes, chairs, stools, tables, or even etch glassware. Experiment and make your stencils big or small, front-on or profile, mirror image or all facing the same way. In the next few crafts, you'll see some of the possibilities.

Difficulty Rating:

TOOLS & MATERIALS

✔ Stencil sheet
✔ Image of dog
✔ Permanent marker
✔ X-Acto knife

Step-by-Step Directions

1. Place the stencil sheet over the image of the dog (see Appendix B on page 149). Using the marker, trace the image.

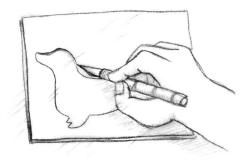

2. Cut out the image with the X-Acto knife.

Hints & Tips

- If you use an X-Acto knife and cut carefully, you can save the inside piece of the stencil and use that to make the reverse image.

BREEDOIDS: 1. Miniature Pinschers, which first came from Germany, move their front and hind legs parallel when they walk, giving them a more wobbly-looking gait. **2.** Faithful owners of **Vizslas** who brought their beloved pets with them when they emigrated from Hungary during World War II are likely the reason the breed exists today.

FACTOID: Dogs have been war heroes for over a century. The first war-dog school was begun in Germany in 1870. Today there are war-dog schools all over the world.

39

Tail-Waggingly Easy Invitation

*T*ail wagging is a divine movement, and my husband speaks of wishing he had a tail to wag every once in a while. My mother has three Bichon Frises at the moment—Casper, Corky, and Collie. For those of you unfamiliar with the breed, Bichons have what are known as *squirrel tails, since the tails curl up and fall on top of the dogs' backs. Mom clips her Bichons' fur really short so she doesn't have to brush them; however, her groomer keeps the hair on Casper's, Corky's, and Collie's tails long. The resulting look is like a trio of cheerleaders. Standing in a row, peering out of their little black eyes past their little black noses, Corky, Casper, and Collie raise their tails a few inches off their backs and madly wag, causing their tail pom-poms to wave. On sight, my husband and I usually pump our arms and yell "Gooo teeeam!" causing their tails to wag even faster. This craft is as easy for humans as tail wagging is for our four-legged pals.*

Difficulty Rating:

TOOLS & MATERIALS

- ✔ White card stock
- ✔ Scissors
- ✔ Envelopes of your choice
- ✔ Your dog stencil (Who Let the Dogs Out? Stencil on page 108)
- ✔ 2B pencil
- ✔ Markers the color of your dog

Step-by-Step Directions

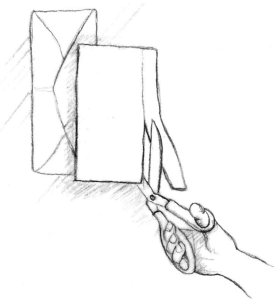

1. Cut a piece of card stock so that it will fit into the envelope. Repeat for as many invitations as you need.

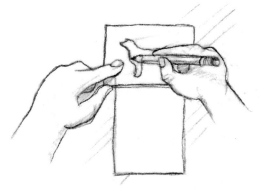

2. Place stencil where you would like the image of the dog to be. Draw the outline of the figure lightly with a pencil.

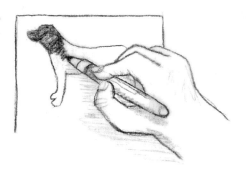

3. Color in the image.

4. Repeat Steps 2 and 3 on all your invitations. Using your pen, write the who, what, where, and when of the festivities.

Hints & Tips

- Consider using decorative scissors, like scalloped, for a different look.
- If you don't have stencils, you can still make this invitation by tracing an image of a dog with a 2B pencil and tracing paper, turning the paper over to superimpose the image onto the card stock, and then coloring in the image using a marker. To superimpose the image, turn over the tracing paper with the traced image and retrace. A faint line will be left on the card stock.

JUST RIGHT

The 125th Westminster Kennel Club Dog Show's Best in Show champion in 2001 was a little Bichon Frise named J. R., or Just Right. He was the most-winning dog (of *all* breeds) for the year 2000 and also the first Bichon to earn Best in Show status at Westminster since the breed was accepted by the AKC in the sixties. Although I am partial to the breed since I own one, we have another connection to Champion J. R. Corky, Collie, and Casper, my mom's dogs, all come from J.R.'s breeder, Ellie McDonald.

However, to create the perfect dog you have to try and try again. Mom's dogs could be named Try, Try Again, and Really, Really Tried. Corky wins in the looks department, but he bites most of Mom's male visitors. Casper is pretty cute, but he has allergies and in itching himself gives himself pinkish orange spots on his legs. And then there's Collie, oh Collie. She's bowlegged, her back legs are too long, her tail sticks straight out like a Pointer's, and she is so naughty.

Alas, my own little Scout is just as inadequate when compared to Champion J. R. Scout has buff-colored splotches on his back, his legs are twice as long as the breed standard, and he's huge (he weighs 25 percent more than the breed standard). And that's just looks. He's a maniacal licker, he walks along the back of couches like a brazen cat, he wants human food so badly he's eaten a corncob, and he would sell me for half a treat any chance he had. But, then again, I hear J. R.'s pretty naughty, too. Scout hasn't gone for my credit cards yet.

Woofer Wrapping Paper and Gift Tags

The concept of this homemade wrapping paper is the same whether you use your Bone and Hydrant Sponge Stamps and tempera paint or your Sammy Stamps and an ink pad. Experiment with colors of paint, size of image, shape, and of course, paper. I love to use the paper workmen lay down to protect floors while painting. It's inexpensive and unrefined, leaving it dappled with specks like handmade paper.

Another favorite paper, especially with dog-related gifts, is newspaper. Cut small pieces of white card stock or a small piece of the same paper to make correlating gift tags.

Paper Using Bone and Hydrant Sponge Stamps

These stamps will have a messier appearance than Sammy Stamps because of the effect of the sponge and the watery paint. Also, some of the stamp images might have holes in them from air bubbles.

Difficulty Rating:

BREEDOID: The hound relatives of the **Beagle,** who were bred to hunt rabbits and hares, have existed since the fourteenth century.

TOOLS & MATERIALS

✔ Newspaper
✔ Bowls with bottoms big enough for your stamp pad to lie flat

✔ Tempera paint: red, white
✔ Bone and Hydrant Sponge Stamps (page 106)

Step-by-Step Directions

1. Give yourself lots of space on the floor and lay out newspaper to protect the area from paint. Lay the newspaper you're going to decorate on top of the protective layer of newspaper.

2. Fill the bottom of each of your bowls with ¼" of tempera paint, one red, one white.

3. Dip your stamp into the bowl and decorate the paper with your stamp pads. Let dry.

Paper Using Sammy Stamps

*T*hese stamp images will look more like the rubber store-bought ones. Be sure to cover the entire stamp with ink and press *down evenly across the whole stamp. The overall effect will be neat and professional if the images are stamped evenly and cleanly.*

Difficulty Rating:

TOOLS & MATERIALS

✔ Sammy Stamps (page 103)
✔ Ink pad
✔ Paper

Step-by-Step Directions

1. Using stamp and ink pad, cover the stamp's image with ink.

2. Press the stamp firmly and evenly on the paper.

3. Repeat in a pattern and let dry.

Hints & Tips

- When letting your paper dry, be sure to keep it off the floor, lest a real dog walk across it—or lie right on top of it!

FACTOID: The first dog to appear on a stamp was a **Newfoundland,** who graced his country's stamp in 1931. Since then dozens of countries have featured dogs on their stamps.

"Pup-Up" Invitation or Greeting Card

*O*f the more than 43 million dog owners in the United States, almost 10 million celebrate their dogs' birthdays, and of that number, almost 1 million give their dogs birthday parties. Poor Scout, so ill-treated and unfed, has only had one birthday party in his four years. It was more of a hit with the humans than the canines, but it was a grand Quasha family event. The guests included Sasha Quasha, a blond Cocker Spaniel, Max Quasha, a fawn Pug, and Sammy Quasha-Temtchine, a mutt extraordinaire. Party highlights included a game of Whoever Sits First Gets a Treat, and the immediate de-eyeing by Max of his gift to Scout, a neon orange, squeaky hedgehog. One of these years we'll have a repeat event, when the humans have recovered.

Difficulty Rating:

TOOLS & MATERIALS

✔ Scissors
✔ 1 piece of white card stock, 8½" x 11"
✔ Sheets of construction paper:
  yellow, red, and green

✔ Envelopes
✔ 2B pencil
✔ Tracing paper
✔ Image of your dog
✔ Markers the color of your dog
✔ Clear tape
✔ Black marker

Step-by-Step Directions

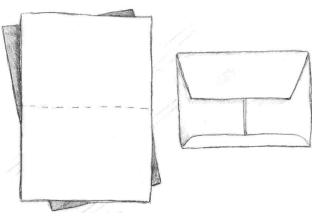

1. Cut the white card stock and yellow construction paper into rectangles that, when folded in half, will fit into your envelopes. Once cut, fold each in half.

2. Take the white card stock and in the center of the crease cut two 1" slits about 1" apart. (This will become your pop up.)

3. Cut a large red bone from the red construction paper and a patch of green grass from the green paper.

4. Using the pencil and tracing paper, trace the image of your dog (see Appendix B on page 149).

5. On the leftover piece of white card stock, turn over the tracing paper and retrace the image of your dog. This should leave a light pencil image.

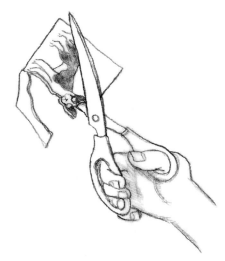

6. Color in your dog with the dog-colored markers and cut the image out.

7. Using the clear tape, tape the bone, grass, and dog to the card stock. Tape the dog to the pop-out slit. Tape the card stock into the yellow construction paper, making sure not to tape down the slit.

8. Write your invitation or greeting card with the black marker.

Pop-Up Dog Bowl Invitation

*F*ollow the same steps as for the "Pup-Up" Invitation or Greeting Card, but use the paper listed below to make a Pop-Up Dog Bowl Invitation. Cut a dog bowl from the red paper, kibble from the brown paper, a candle from the green paper, and a flame from the yellow paper. I used blue paper for the outside of the card.

Difficulty Rating:

TOOLS & MATERIALS

✔ Scissors
✔ 1 piece of white card stock, 8½" x 11"
✔ Sheets of construction paper: brown, green, red, yellow, and blue
✔ Envelopes
✔ Clear tape
✔ Black marker

Hints & Tips

- I have included the bare-minimum tools for this craft. Consider using more colored construction paper or glitter to add a bit more glamour.
- Make sure when you close your pop-up card that the pop-up portion does not extend further than the edge of the paper; otherwise it won't fit into the envelope.

> **BREEDOID:** The **Boston Terrier,** once called the Yankee Terrier and the Boston Gentleman, is one of America's only native breeds.

Ode to Toupee Drink Coasters

In the late fifties, my grandfather brought home a black Miniature Poodle for my dad, my uncle, and my aunt, who were ten, eight, and seven years old. The three couldn't believe their luck. They immediately fell in love with the pup and named him Toupee. Toupee was not the brightest pooch in the pound, nor, it turned out, was he miniature. He kept on growing, and Toupee went from Miniature to Standard before he was done. However, although Toupee's body kept growing, his brain did not. Every Sunday the family (mom, dad, and the three children), all properly dressed, sitting up straight, and under my grandfather's strict watch, gathered to watch an hour of television "as a family." Their TV was one of those furniture TVs—a massive piece that took up a whole wall, stood on the floor, and was actually a sideboard, shelves, and TV all in one. Without fail, every time the family settled onto the couch to watch Family Television, Toupee would lie down in front of the TV, raise his left leg, and noisily clean himself. Outraged at the barbarity, my grandfather would leap up from his wing chair, shake his right fist high in the air, and scream "Toupee!" Always stunned at my grand-

dad's explosion, Toupee would jump to all fours and flee the room, sometimes leaving a stream of piddle behind him. A string of quasi profanities would fly from my grandfather's mouth as he stood in the door frame red in the face, while my grandmother, dad, uncle, and aunt tried desperately to quash their giggles. No sooner would my grandfather sit back down than Toupee would tiptoe back in and lie down in front of the TV to resume his cleaning.

I grew up loving this story and the memory of Toupee, and my dad has probably recounted the tale a hundred times. Every time he does, he laughs until he's red in the face and it brings tears to his eyes. All those suppressed giggles have finally been freed.

I can see these drink coasters in that room—except I promise that these dogs will be well-behaved. Make them as subtle or outrageous as you want. For the subtle look try cutting out images of silver dog jewelry and gluing them between circles of tracing paper. The images of the dogs *will be visible, but the overall effect will be uniform and faint. It would also be fun to make a set of coasters where each one is a close-up of a dog's face taken with a telephoto lens, so that the dog's nose is much bigger than the rest of its face.*

Difficulty Rating:

TOOLS & MATERIALS

✔ 4 images of dogs from magazines
   or catalogs
✔ Scissors
✔ Colored paper
✔ Rubber cement or glue stick
✔ Access to a laminator (most
   photo-developing shops have them)

Step-by-Step Directions

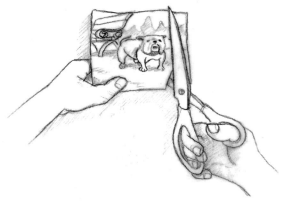

1. Cut out or photocopy 4 images of dogs from a magazine or catalog.

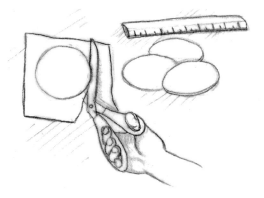

2. Cut out four 4" circles from the colored paper.

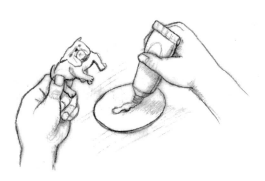

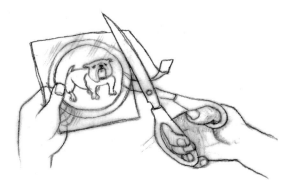

3. Glue the 4 images onto the 4 round pieces of paper. Laminate the 4 circles, or have them laminated for you.

4. Cut out the circles from the lamination, leaving at least ¼" around the colored paper.

Hints & Tips

- Consider using leftover wallpaper or wrapping paper for the background.
- Also consider using fancy scissors that have a scalloped edge to make the background circle.
- These drink coasters make great (and easy) holiday and housewarming gifts.
- You can also glue, using fabric glue, a 3" circle of felt or a thin layer of corkboard to the back of each laminated coaster.

BREEDOIDS: 1. Charly, a **French Poodle**, stars in the beloved book by John Steinbeck, *Travels with Charly*. **2. Dachshunds** are bred in two sizes: standard and miniature. **3. Bichons** can be found in paintings by the Spanish painter Goya. **4.** Bred for bullbaiting, the **Bulldog**'s strong jaw allowed him to bite his enemy and hold on tightly.

PART

The Holidays Have Gone to the Dogs

Festive Fido Decorations

SIX

A Holiday Dog Breed Ornament

When my mother was pregnant with me she made more than a dozen felt ornaments for our Christmas tree of characters from fairy tales and stories that I would one day read. From my very first Christmas tree, I grew up with Goldilocks, Mama Bear, Papa Bear, and Baby Bear; Dorothy, the Cowardly Lion, the Tin Man, and the Scarecrow (where was Toto?); Raggedy Ann and Andy; and Hansel and Gretel gently swaying from our Christmas tree. Pet ornaments make perfect holiday gifts as well as a tangible lasting memory of a favorite pet. There is no reason you can't stitch your pet's name onto the backside or frontside of the ornament.

Difficulty Rating:

TOOLS & MATERIALS

✔ White paper
✔ 2B pencil
✔ Scissors
✔ Pins

✔ 2 8" x 11" pieces of dog-colored felt
✔ Colored embroidery or regular thread
✔ Needle
✔ Small bells
✔ Polyester fill
✔ Colored ribbon
✔ Buttons for eyes
✔ Gold thread or thin gold ribbon

Step-by-Step Directions

1. Using the white paper and a pencil, draw the image of your pet, or copy it from the back of the book (see Appendix B on page 149). Cut it out.

2. Pin the paper image onto two pieces of felt. Cut around the paper image, through the felt, creating two shapes of your pet from the felt. Remove the paper from the felt.

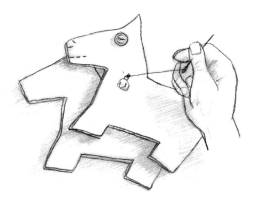

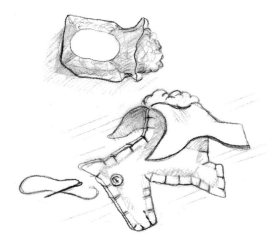

3. On the piece of felt that will make the front of the ornament, use embroidery or regular thread to sew on the button eyes and bell, and create the nose and mouth with stitches.

4. Using a blanket stitch, sew around the edge, stuffing the ornament with polyester fill as you go.

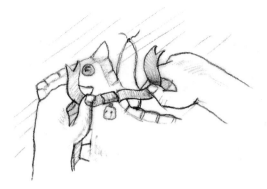

5. Tie ribbon around the ornament's neck above the bell. Add gold thread for hanging the ornament by threading one end through a blanket stitch on top of the ornament. Tie the ends of the gold thread into a knot to hang.

Hints & Tips

- When drawing your ornament on the paper, make the image of your pet bigger than you might initially think you should. When you add the stitches and use poly-fill the ornament will "shrink" because of the added volume. This is especially true when cutting out tails, ears, and paws. The extra space will allow you more room to stuff them.
- Don't wait until after you have filled and sewn up the ornament to attach eyes and sew the mouth. It is much

more difficult to hide the stitches at this stage.

- Start your blanket stitch in a crevice, for example, where the tail or paw meets the body. This will draw less attention to the knot. Also, aim to start sewing at the bottom of the ornament rather than the top. Again, the knot will draw less attention there.
- Stuff your ornament as you sew around it. Don't wait until you are almost through sewing to start putting poly-fill into it.
- Leave enough space, either over or under the bell, to tie on the ribbon.

Too-Proud-to-Beg
Bone Ornament

Difficulty Rating:

TOOLS & MATERIALS

✔ 2B pencil
✔ Red felt
✔ Scissors
✔ White embroidery thread
✔ Needle
✔ 6 white buttons
✔ Polyester fill
✔ Gold thread or thin gold ribbon

Step-by-Step Directions

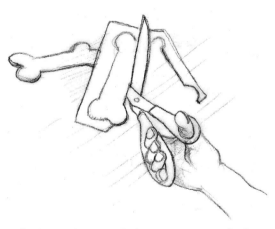

1. Using the pencil, draw an image of a bone on the red felt. Cut it out. Using the cut-out bone from the felt, trace another bone image onto the red felt and cut it out. This will make two identical bones.

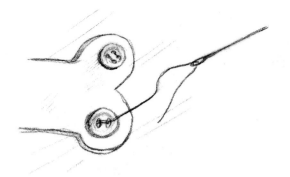

2. On the piece of felt that will make the front of the ornament, use the white embroidery thread to sew on the buttons.

3. Place the two pieces of felt on top of each other. Using a blanket stitch, sew around the edge, stuffing the ornament with polyester fill as you go.

4. Add gold thread for hanging the ornament by threading one end through a blanket stitch on top of the ornament. Tie the ends of the gold thread into a knot to hang.

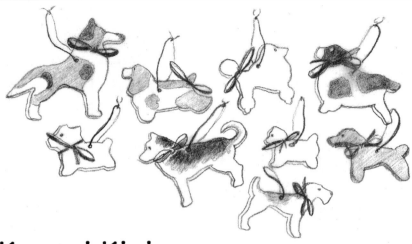

Kennel Klub Kristmas Ornaments

In my previous life when I worked in an office, Scout went to Sutton Dog Parlor's Playcare three days a week. He was part of a group of around twenty small dogs who romped indoors most of the time, but who were let out back behind the brownstone a few times a day to do their business. Because this playtime began when Scout was only a few months old, he's very social, both with humans and with other dogs. He loved it. Every time I brought him to Sutton, Scout always pulled me toward the back (away from the grooming area) where the playing happened.

About three years into it, one day upon picking Scout up, Albert, a longtime Sutton employee, walkie-talkied the guy out back and said, "We need Trouble to be brought up front." Albert, a rather quiet, almost downtrodden fellow who occasionally breaks into wide mustachioed grins, looked at me sheepishly. "What's that all about?" I asked with a smile, wondering about the nickname they had devised for Scout. He waited a second before speaking. "Oh my God," he said, shaking his head. "Your dog, he causes so much trouble." Really? I thought. And this was the first I was hearing of it? "What does he do?" I asked, fearing his day care days might be over. "He spends the whole day humping other dogs," Albert replied. No wonder Scout loves playtime so much. I bet he wants me back in an office job.

Difficulty Rating:

TOOLS & MATERIALS

✔ Wax paper
✔ Self-drying clay
✔ Rolling pin or wine bottle
✔ Dog-shaped cookie cutters
✔ Bowl of water
✔ Wooden skewer
✔ Paintbrushes
✔ Clay sealer
✔ Acrylic paint the colors of your
   dog
✔ Water-based acrylic urethane
   gloss
✔ Gold thread
✔ Ribbon
✔ Cooling rack

Step-by-Step Directions

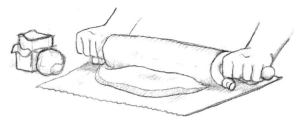

1. On top of the wax paper, place a fist-sized ball of clay. Using a rolling pin or a wine bottle with no label, roll the clay until it is flat and about ¼" thick.

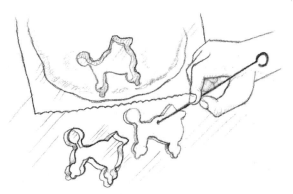

2. Press dog cookie cutters into the clay and pull out. Remove the clay from the cutter. Using a dab of water on your fingertip, fix any spots or lines on the clay. Using wooden skewer, poke a hole in the ornament. Let dry on a cooling rack.

3. Using a paintbrush, place a coat of clay sealer on both sides of the dog. Let dry.

131

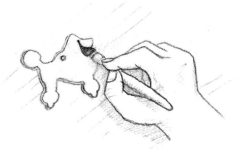

4. Using acrylic paint, paint your dog, and repeat as many times as necessary. Paint on eyes. Let dry.

5. Paint a layer of water-based glaze over your dog.

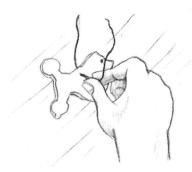

6. Tie a loop through the hole with gold thread to make the dog into a hanging ornament. Add ribbon collar.

Hints & Tips

- Don't let the clay sit on the wax paper too long as the moisture of the clay dissolves the wax paper, making it stick to the clay.
- You can skip the sealer step, but it's better not to.

BREEDOIDS: 1. There are three sizes of **Schnauzer:** miniature, standard, and giant. The standard is the oldest, dating back to the fifteenth century, and the youngest is the miniature, who was only bred at the turn of the twentieth century. **2.** The **Collie's** name comes from the name of the black sheep it once herded in Scotland, who were known as "coalies." **3.** The **Yorkshire Terrier's** original use was to escort miners into the depths of the earth to kill rats. **4.** Many **Airedale Terriers** worked as messengers in both World War I and World War II.

FACTOID: *Lassie Come Home* was first a short story written in 1938 by Eric Knight. It then became a novel, and it finally reached the big screen in 1943.

Paw Print Ornament

I love Scout's paws, and when Irene Hecht, an animal portraitist in New York, painted Scout, she was sure to include the one pink toe on Scout's right hind paw for me. I like to check out Scout's paws occasionally, look at them, poke around, see if it's all okay in there. However, Scout hates having his paws touched. He looks at me with the bored-teenager look and I imagine him thinking, "Oh jeez, Mom's touching my paws again." Whichever one I'm holding, he pulls it away. I try to take hold of it again. He pulls it away again. He gets up and walks away. Sometimes I get up and follow him. It continues until one of us gets tired, and then the other one wins.

This is a terrific craft to do with kids, and, with Scout as my proof, you don't even need a patient dog to do it with. The results are fun, and the kid-friendly molding clay won't stick to your dog's paw or fur. These paw print molds are also very light when they dry, unlike other clays.

Difficulty Rating:

TOOLS & MATERIALS

✔ Self-drying, spongy "model magic clay" for kids
✔ Your dog
✔ Embroidery needle
✔ Gold embroidery thread

BREEDOIDS: 1. Rottweilers were bred in Rottweil, Germany, to herd cattle and for protection, and today it continues to be the most popular guard dog in America. **2. Great Pyrenees** were bred to protect and move flocks of sheep around the Pyrenees Mountains, and it much prefers to live in wide open spaces.

Step-by-Step Directions

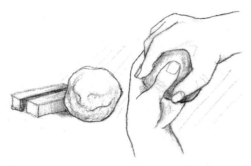

1. Roll a chunk of model magic clay the size of a golf ball into a ball. (If you have a big dog, you may need a little more, and if you have a small dog, you might not need as much.)

2. Slightly flatten the clay with the palm of your hand.

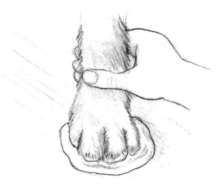

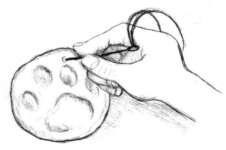

3. Take your dog's paw and press it down into the clay. Make sure you press all the dog's "toes" firmly into the clay. Let dry.

4. Thread your needle with the embroidery thread and sew a piece of gold thread through the top of the dry paw print. (FYI: You won't be able to sew through "regular" clay.)

Hints & Tips

- The best results come when you put the clay on the floor and your dog steps onto it. Gravity helps give a consistent imprint, and the floor gives the ornament a nice flat back.

FACTOID: Did you know that a twelve-thousand-year-old skeleton of a woman was found in Israel with her hand resting on the body of her dog?

Putting on
the Pooch

For Dog Lovers

on the Move

47

A-OK Dog Tag Earrings

*Y*ou don't have to buy new dog tags to make this craft, but to match an outfit, you can find every color of the rainbow out there. If your vet is as nice as mine is and gives you old tags, make sure you hold up your end of the bargain. Old dog tags are often sought by dog owners who have not vaccinated their pet but still want the pet to look like it has been vaccinated. This, of course, is illegal, and since your vet's name is on the tags, he or she could get into trouble—so don't let them fall into the wrong paws. If you are one of those people who is always losing earrings, make sure you lose these earrings in a safe place!

Difficulty Rating:

TOOLS & MATERIALS

✔ Needle-nosed or regular pliers
✔ 2 ear wires or 2 fishhook ear wires
✔ 2 dog tags

Step-by-Step Directions

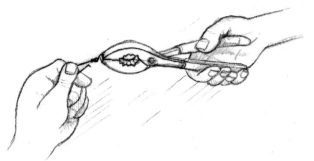

1. With the pliers, bend an ear wire hoop to an open position.

2. Slide on one dog tag. Be sure that the front of the tag is facing out, so it can be seen when the earring is on.

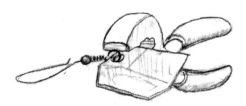

3. With the pliers, close the hoop tightly. Repeat for the second earring.

BREEDOIDS: 1. Papillon means "butterfly" in French, and the breed was likely named thus because its ears look like butterfly wings. **2.** Because of their size and appearance, **Mastiffs** have been considered mascots of war and sometimes have even been adorned in armor.

FACTOID: Visit your vet annually, not just when your dog gets sick.

Dog-Button Earrings and Brooch

W ho says you can't have affordable gold or silver dog earrings that look good above your fanciest suit or your velvet holiday dress? These earrings are no-brainers once you find your buttons. Check out my sources in the back of the book to find the perfect dog buttons for you.

Difficulty Rating:

TOOLS & MATERIALS

✔ Wire cutters
✔ 2 dog buttons
✔ Quick-drying, strong household glue
✔ 2 clip-on or stud earring backs

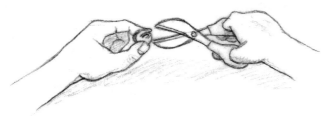

1. If necessary, take the wire cutters and cut off the buttonhole hoop on the back of each of the buttons. (If your buttons have their holes through them, rather than behind them, you can skip this step.) Consider how and where you want the button to be glued to the earring back.

2. Place a dab of glue on the back of each button and affix to the earring back. Hold together and wait until it dries slightly, and then let it rest to dry fully.

Dog-Button Brooch

*F*ancy brooches can be expensive, but not if you make one out of a large button. They make great gifts. Make sure you choose a button that is at least an inch wide.

Difficulty Rating:

Step-by-Step Directions

1. If necessary, take the wire cutters and cut off the buttonhole hoop on the back of your button. (If your buttons have their holes through them, rather than behind them, you can skip this step.) Consider how and where you want the button to be glued.

2. Place a dab of glue on the back of the button and glue it to the bar pin. Hold it together until it dries slightly, and then let it rest to dry fully.

TOOLS & MATERIALS

✔ Wire cutters
✔ 1 dog button, at least 1" wide
✔ Quick-drying, strong household glue
✔ Bar pin

FACTOID: A five-story brownstone on New York City's East Side plays host to the Leash, a private club founded in 1925 for dog breeders and fanciers.

49

Sighing Dog Brooches

*D*on't you love it when your dog is lying at your feet and, after lounging in the same position for over an hour, he suddenly moves, causing you to look down? Then, after a slight movement, such as shifting his hind leg or moving his jowl half an inch, he takes a deep breath and lets out a big sigh. "Hah-rumph."

Such is the life of a dog. The effort of changing a lounge position calls for a deep sigh. It always makes me smile and reflect on how I'd like to come back as a well-fed, well-loved dog the next time around.

Here's how to make your own sighing dog. He'll just lie there, pinned to your chest, causing very little disturbance whatsoever.

Difficulty Rating:

TOOLS & MATERIALS

✔ Wax paper
✔ Self-drying clay
✔ Rolling pin or wine bottle
✔ Dog cookie cutters

✔ Bowl of water
✔ Paintbrushes
✔ Clay sealer
✔ Acrylic paint
✔ Water-based acrylic urethane gloss
✔ Strong household glue
✔ Bar pins
✔ Red, blue, yellow, or green ribbon
✔ Cooling rack

Step-by-Step Directions

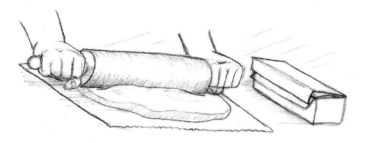

1. On top of the wax paper, place a fist-sized ball of clay. Using a rolling pin or a wine bottle with no label, roll the clay until it is flat and about ¼" thick.

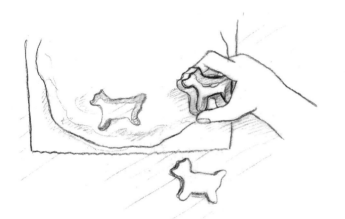

2. Press dog cookie cutters into the clay and pull out. Remove the clay figure from the cookie cutter. Using a dab of water on your fingertip, fix any spots or lines on the clay. Let dry on a cooling rack.

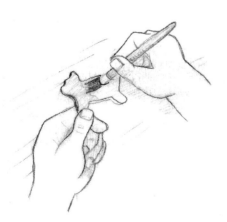

3. Using a paintbrush, place a coat of sealer on both sides of the dog. Let dry.

4. Paint your dog with acrylic paint, and repeat as many times as necessary. Let dry.

5. Paint a layer of water-based gloss over your dog.

- Don't let the clay sit on the wax paper too long as the moisture of the clay dissolves the wax paper, making it stick to the clay.
- You can skip the sealer step, but I don't recommend it.
- Let the glue dry a bit before sticking the bar pin to the clay figure. This allows the bar pin to "rest" in the glue once it is dry.

6. Using strong glue, stick on bar pin and let dry.

FACTOID: The American Kennel Club Library in New York was established in 1934, and it now houses over sixteen thousand dog-related volumes, three hundred videos, and 250 periodicals.

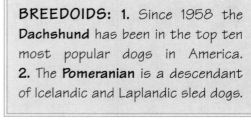

BREEDOIDS: 1. Since 1958 the **Dachshund** has been in the top ten most popular dogs in America. **2.** The **Pomeranian** is a descendant of Icelandic and Laplandic sled dogs.

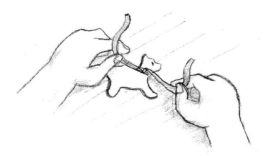

7. Tie ribbon around the neck to make the collar.

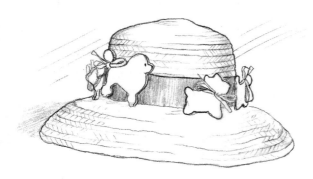

Dog-Chase Garden Hat

When Scout is hanging out with his three Bichon cousins in the country, I love to be the one who lets the four of them outside to play. After I make the appropriate sound the four of them race to the door, and eagerly jump up and down on their hind legs, dying to be let out. Each wants to be the first one out, the first one to chase the squirrel, the first one to mark a particular shrub. Once the door is opened, four white spots dash across the bright green lawn. Collie, the one female and the puppy, is always being chased by the others, and she loves it. Scout, who has a thing for other small white dogs, is her biggest admirer. Darting left and right, right and left, young dog energy is a treat to watch. These forays into my mom's backyard inspired this colorful hat.

Whether clipping your backyard roses, reading on the beach, or heading to a summer wedding, this adorable hat will let people know where your priorities lie. You can also employ the brooches separately; however, this dog chase is tough to break up.

Difficulty Rating:

TOOLS & MATERIALS

- ✔ 1 yard of red grosgrain ribbon, 1½" thick
- ✔ Garden hat
- ✔ Scissors
- ✔ Needle
- ✔ Red thread
- ✔ 6 brooch pins (see Sighing Dog Brooches craft, page 141)

Step-by-Step Directions

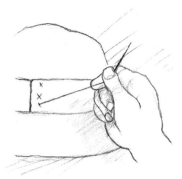

1. Wrap the grosgrain ribbon around the hat, and cut ribbon to the desired length.

2. Using needle and thread, make three small stitches to hold each end of the ribbon together and in place on the hat.

3. Pin the brooches to the ribbon around the hat.

BREEDOIDS: 1. One of the early "official" breeds, **Dachshunds** were recorded in a stud book in 1840. **2.** Not surprisingly, the **Pomeranian**, one of the most toylike breeds, is a member of the toy group. **3. Cairn Terriers** often live to be fourteen years old and make great companion dogs.

FACTOID: The Dog Rose might have been named because the ancient Greeks thought it was able to heal dog bites.

Appendix A: Top Dog Breeds

The following is a current list of top dog breeds, as ranked by registration, from the American Kennel Club (AKC).

1. Labrador Retriever
2. Golden Retriever
3. German Shepherd
4. Dachshund
5. Beagle
6. Poodle
7. Yorkshire Terrier
8. Chihuahua
9. Boxer
10. Shih Tzu
11. Rottweiler
12. Pomeranian
13. Miniature Schnauzer
14. Cocker Spaniel
15. Pug
16. Shetland Sheepdog
17. Miniature Pinscher
18. Boston Terrier
19. Siberian Husky
20. Maltese
21. Bulldog
22. Basset Hound
23. Doberman Pinscher
24. German Shorthaired Pointer
25. Bichon Frise
26. English Springer Spaniel
27. Pembroke Welsh Corgi
28. Great Dane
29. Pekingese
30. West Highland White Terrier
31. Brittany
32. Weimaraner
33. Lhasa Apso
34. Collie
35. Australian Shepherd
36. Saint Bernard
37. Chinese Shar-Pei
38. Akita
39. Mastiff
40. Cairn Terrier
41. Chesapeake Bay Retriever
42. Scottish Terrier
43. Papillon
44. Chow Chow
45. Great Pyrenees
46. Airedale Terrier
47. Vizsla
48. Alaskan Malamute
49. Dalmatian
50. Bloodhound
51. Italian Greyhound
52. Bullmastiff
53. Newfoundland
54. Cavalier King Charles Spaniel
55. Shiba Inu
56. Soft Coated Wheaten Terrier
57. Rhodesian Ridgeback
58. Bernese Mountain Dog
59. Samoyed
60. Schipperke
61. Silky Terrier
62. Irish Setter
63. Whippet
64. Border Collie
65. American Staffordshire Terrier
66. Old English Sheepdog
67. Australian Cattle Dog
68. Wire Fox Terrier
69. Chinese Crested
70. Basenji
71. French Bulldog
72. Jack Russell Terrier
73. German Wirehaired Pointer
74. Japanese Chin
75. Keeshond
76. English Cocker Spaniel
77. Bouvier des Flandres
78. Bull Terrier
79. Brussels Griffon
80. Portuguese Water Dog
81. Cardigan Welsh Corgi
82. Norwegian Elkhound
83. Giant Schnauzer
84. Gordon Setter

85. Irish Wolfhound
86. Havanese
87. Borzoi
88. Afghan Hound
89. Border Terrier
90. Tibetan Terrier
91. English Setter
92. Beardie Collie
93. Smooth Fox Terrier
94. Welsh Terrier
95. Belgian Malinois
96. Standard Schnauzer
97. Staffordshire Bull Terrier
98. Flat-Coated Retriever
99. American Eskimo Dog
100. Pointer
101. Australian Terrier
102. Norwich Terrier
103. Tibetan Spaniel
104. Greater Swiss Mountain Dog
105. Manchester Terrier
106. Belgian Tervuren

107. Kerry Blue Terrier
108. Belgian Sheepdog
109. Saluki
110. Briard
111. Irish Terrier
112. Wirehaired Pointing Griffon
113. Welsh Springer Spaniel
114. Petit Basset Griffon Vendeen
115. Norfolk Terrier
116. English Toy Spaniel
117. Affenpinscher
118. Greyhound
119. Lakeland Terrier
120. Kuvasz
121. Clumber Spaniel
122. Black and Tan Coonhound
123. Anatolian Shepherd Dog
124. Bedlington Terrier
125. American Water Spaniel
126. Irish Water Spaniel
127. Scottish Deerhound

128. Miniature Bull Terrier
129. Puli
130. Polish Lowland Sheepdog
131. Curly-Coated Retriever
132. Lowchen
133. Plott Coonhound
134. Field Spaniel
135. Komondor
136. Ibizan Hound
137. Skye Terrier
138. Dandie Dinmont Terrier
139. Pharaoh Hound
140. Canaan Dog
141. Finnish Spitz
142. American Foxhound
143. Sussex Spaniel
144. Sealyham Terrier
145. Spinone Italiano
146. Otterhound
147. Harrier
148. English Foxhound

Appendix B: Tracing Outlines of the Top 50 Dog Breeds

The following list of dogs is arranged alphabetically. Use and adapt these drawings to suit your project. If your dog is not included, and you don't have an image handy, try looking for a good picture in a dog encyclopedia.

1. Airedale Terrier

2. Akita

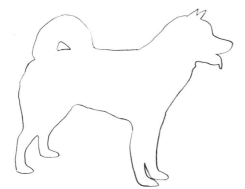

3. Alaskan Malamute

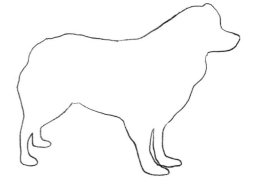

4. Australian Shepherd

5. Basset Hound

6. Beagle

7. Bichon Frise

8. Boston Terrier

9. Boxer

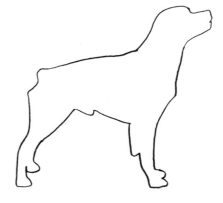

10. Brittany

11. Bulldog

12. Cairn Terrier

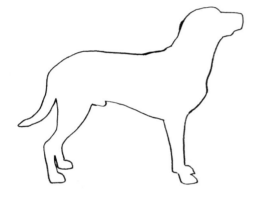

13. Chesapeake Bay Retriever

14. Chihuahua

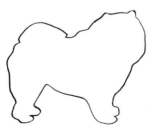

15. Chow Chow

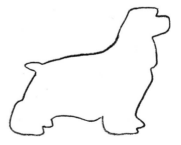

16. Cocker Spaniel

17. Collie

18. Corgi

19. Dachshund

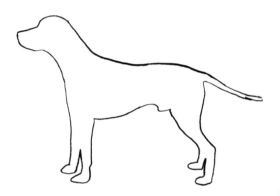

20. Dalmatian

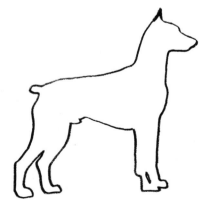

21. Doberman Pinscher

22. English Springer Spaniel

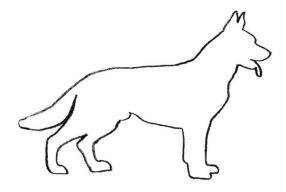

23. German Shepherd

24. Golden Retriever

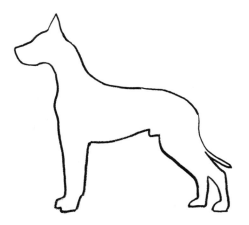

25. Great Dane

26. Great Pyrenees

27. Husky

28. Jack Russell Terrier

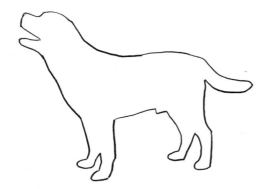

29. Labrador Retriever

30. Lhasa Apso

31. Maltese

32. Mastiff

33. Miniature Pinscher

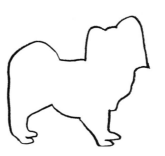

34. Papillon

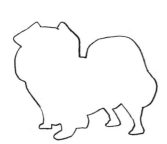

35. Pekingese

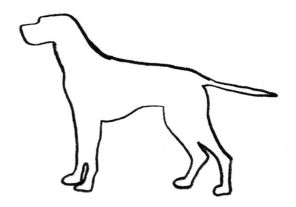

36. Pointer

37. Pomeranian

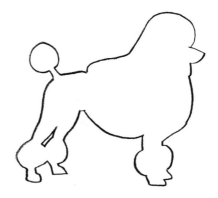

38. Poodle

39. Pug

40. Rottweiler

41. Saint Bernard

42. Schnauzer

43. Scottish Terrier

44. Shar-Pei

45. Shetland Sheepdog

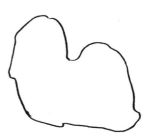

46. Shih Tzu

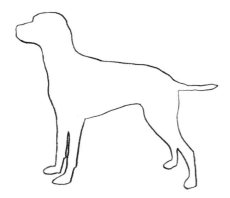

47. Vizsla

48. Weimaraner

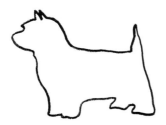

49. West Highland White Terrier

50. Yorkshire Terrier

Appendix C: Listing and Images of Selected Dog Breeds and Related Craft Projects

The following list is alphabetical by breed. Numbers in parentheses indicate the project number or numbers for the crafts in the book where the breed is represented. Dog breeds in bold type are illustrated by drawings on the pages that follow.

Airedale Terrier (45) Kennel Klub Kristmas Ornaments

Akita (7) Our Doghouse Placard

Alaskan Malamute (15) Dog Phrase Napkin Rings

Australian Shepherd (3) Bone Doormat

Basset Hound (1) Fido Finials, (20) Best-in-Show Lazy Susan

Beagle (21) Dog Tag Picture Frame, (40) Woofer Wrapping Paper and Gift Tags

Bichon Frise (43) A Holiday Dog Breed Ornament, (13) Mug-for-Me Decoupage Plates, (42) Ode to Toupee Drink Coasters

Boston Terrier (41) "Pup-Up" Invitation or Greeting Card

Boxer (10) Dog Run Corkboard

Brittany (4) Retriever Message Board

Brussels Griffon (27) Royal Pug Pillows

Bull Mastiff/Mastiff (47) A-OK Dog Tag Earrings

Bulldog (8) Kanine Key Hooks, (42) Ode to Toupee Drink Coasters

Cairn Terriers (50) Dog-Chase Garden Hat

Cardigan Welsh Corgi (8) Kanine Key Hooks, (20) Best-in-Show Lazy Susan

Cavalier King Charles Spaniel (9) Dogs-in-Art Tissue Box Cover

Chesapeake Bay Retriever (3) Bone Doormat

Chihuahua (14) Give-a-Dog-a-Bone Place Mats

Chow Chow (17) Lucky's Luminary

Cocker Spaniel (5) The Tassel That Wags the Dog

Collie (45) Kennel Klub Kristmas Ornaments

Dachshund (23) Pet Silhouette, (1) Fido Finials, (14) Give-a-Dog-a-Bone Place Mats, (49) Sighing Dog Brooches, (50) Dog-Chase Garden Hat, (42) Ode to Toupee Drink Coasters

Dalmatian (12) Lyin' Dog Place Card Holders

Doberman Pinscher (36) Sammy Stamps

English Springer Spaniel (1) Fido Finials, (4) Retriever Message Board, (48) Dog-Button Earrings and Brooch

German Shepherd (8) Kanine Key Hooks, (45) Kennel Klub Khristmas Ornaments

Golden Retriever (36) Sammy Stamps, (6) Fetch, Run, Catch, Play! Tic-Tac-Toe Board

Great Dane (35) Antique Dog-Button Pillow

Great Pyrenees (46) Paw Print Ornament

Husky (34) Single Breed Sachets

Irish Setter (36) Sammy Stamps

Jack Russell Terrier (37) Bone and Hydrant Sponge Stamp

Labrador Retriever (12) Lyin' Dog Place Card Holders, (14) Give-a-Dog-a-Bone Place Mats

Lhasa Apso (28) Hugo's Dog-Bone Button Pillow

Maltese (31) Your-Dog-Here Pillow

Miniature Pinscher (38) Who Let the Dogs Out? Stencils

Newfoundland (40) Woofer Wrapping Paper and Gift Tags

Norfolk/Norwich Terrier (37) Bone and Hydrant Sponge Stamps

Old English Sheepdog (8) Kanine Key Hooks, (20) Best-in-Show Lazy Susan

Papillon (47) A-OK Dog Tag Earrings

Pekingese (28) Hugo's Dog-Bone Button Pillow

Pointer (7) Our Doghouse Placard

Pomeranian (49) Sighing Dog Brooches, (50) Dog-Chase Garden Hat

Poodle (23) Pet Silhouette, (42) Ode to Toupee Drink Coasters

Pug (26 & 27) Pugs & Pillows, (13) Mug-for-Me Decoupage Plates

Rottweiler (46) Paw Print Ornament

Saint Bernard (16) No-Drool Napkins

Schnauzer (45) Kennel Klub Kristmas Ornaments

Scottish Terrier (43) A Holiday Dog Breed Ornament, (30) Scottie Pillowcase, (23) Pet Silhouette

Shar-Pei (17) Lucky's Luminary

Shetland Sheepdog (18) Paw Print Magnets

Shih Tzu (22) A Frame Good Enough to Eat

Vizsla (38) Who Let the Dogs Out? Stencils

Weimaraner (20) Best-in-Show Lazy Susan

West Highland White Terrier (14) Give-a-Dog-a-Bone Place Mats

Yorkshire Terrier (45) Kennel Klub Kristmas Ornaments

Akita

Alaskan Malamute

Australian Shepherd

Basset Hound

Beagle

Bichon Frise

Boxer

Brittany

Brussels Griffon

Bulldog

Cairn Terrier

Cardigan Welsh Corgi

Cavalier King
Charles Spaniel

Chesapeake Bay Retriever

Chihuahua

Chow Chow

Cocker Spaniel

Collie

Dachshund

Dalmatian

Doberman Pinscher

English Springer Spaniel

German Shepherd

Golden Retriever

Great Dane

Great Pyrenees

Husky

163

Jack Russell Terrier   Labrador Retriever   Lhasa Apso

Miniature Pinscher   Newfoundland   Norfolk/Norwich Terrier

Old English Sheepdog   Papillon   Pekingese

Pointer

Pomeranian

Rottweiler

Saint Bernard

Schnauzer

Shar-Pei

Shetland Sheepdog

Shih Tzu

Vizsla

Weimaraner

Yorkshire Terrier

Sources

PART ONE: Doggie-Chic Interior Design: Home Decor Starring Your Dog

1. Fido Finials: miniature dog breeds from Hagen-Renaker, San Mateo, CA, (888) 643-9134, www.hagen-renaker-sales.com; brass finial from Grand Brass Lamp Parts, Inc., New York, NY www.grandbrass.com, (212) 226-2567.
2. Wipe Your Paws! Doormat: coir mat, paint, and brushes from Pergament, Route 119, White Plains, NY, (914) 761-2800.
3. Bone Doormat: coir mat, paint, and brushes from Pergament, Route 119, White Plains, NY, (914) 761-2800.
4. Retriever Message Board: lumber from Century Lumber, 1875 Second Avenue, New York, NY 10029, (212) 876-5439; fabric from Brunschwig & Fils (through decorators); ribbon from M & J Trimmings, 1008 Sixth Avenue (at 38th Street), New York, NY 10018, (212) 391-9072, www.mjtrim.com; upholstery tacks from Kmart, Bridgehampton Commons, Bridgehampton, NY 11932, (631) 537-6449.
5. The Tassel That Wags the Dog: decorative tassel from Paterson Silks, 156 East 86th Street, New York, NY 10028, (212) 722-4384 or (800) 522-5671.
6. Fetch, Run, Catch, Play! Tic-Tac-Toe Board: clay, paint, and brush from Michael's Arts and Crafts, 535 stores nationwide, www.michaels.com; glaze from Janovic Plaza, 1150 Third Avenue, New York, NY 10021, (212) 772-1400.
7. Our Doghouse Placard: balsa wood and paint from Michael's Arts and Crafts, 535 stores nationwide, www.michaels.com.
8. Kanine Key Hooks: paint and brushes from Michael's Arts and Crafts, 535 stores nationwide, www.michaels.com; lumber from Century Lumber, 1875 Second Avenue, New York, NY 10029, (212) 876-5439; screw hooks from Kmart, Bridgehampton Commons, Bridgehampton, NY 11932, (631) 537-6449.
9. Dogs-in-Art Tissue Box Cover: brown cardboard tissue box from AI Freidman, 431 Boston Post Road, Port Chester, NY 10573, (914) 937-7351; dog art images from William Doyle Dogs Auction catalog, William Doyle Gallery, 175 East 87th Street, New York, NY 10128, (212) 427-4141, www.doylenewyork.com (annual auction in February).
10. Dog Run Corkboard: lumber from Century Lumber, 1875 Second Avenue, New York, NY 10029, (212) 876-5439; corkboard from a hardware store; paint from Barney's Place, 107 Greenwich Avenue, Greenwich, CT 06830, (203) 661-7369; dog images from magazines; decoupage glaze from Michael's Arts and Crafts, 535 stores nationwide, www.michaels.com.
11. Bone Bales: metal containers from TJ Maxx, Bridgehampton Commons, Bridgehampton, NY 11932, (631) 537-1591; spray paint from Kmart, Bridgehampton Commons, Bridgehampton, NY 11932, (631) 537-6449; book of ads from 1902 Sears & Roebuck catalog from a used bookstore; gold paint from AI Freidman, 431 Boston Post Road, Port Chester, NY 10573, (914) 937-7351.

PART TWO: All Paws on the Table: Tabletop Decorations Featuring Fido and His Friends

12. Lyin' Dog Place Card Holders: clay, paint, and paintbrushes from AI Freidman, 431 Boston Post Road, Port Chester, NY 10573, (914) 937-7351.

13. Mug-for-Me Decoupage Plates: plates from Lechters; glass paint from AI Freidman, 431 Boston Post Road, Port Chester, NY 10573, (914) 937-7351.

14. Give-a-Dog-a-Bone Place Mats: floor cloth, paint, and paintbrushes from Michael's Arts and Crafts, 535 stores nationwide, www.michaels.com.

15. Dog Phrase Napkin Rings: napkin rings from Michael's Arts and Crafts, 535 stores nationwide, www.michaels.com.

16. No-Drool Napkins: fabric from B&J Fabrics, 263 West 40th (between 7th and 8th Avenues), New York, NY 10018, (212) 354-8150.

17. Lucky's Luminary: this craft uses only household items.

18. Paw Print Magnets: magnets, glass gems, and colorful paper from Michael's Arts and Crafts, 535 stores nationwide, www.michaels.com; black paper from Kate's Paperie, 1282 Third Avenue, New York, NY 10012, (212) 941-9816.

19. Poochie-Poo Pitcher Protector: white fabric from Regent Fabrics, 221 East 60th Street, New York, NY 10022, (212) 355-2039; metal dog charms from M & J Buttons, 1000 Sixth Avenue, New York, NY 10018, (212) 391-6200.

20. Best-in-Show Lazy Susan: lazy Susan from Lechters #513, Kohl's Shopping Center, Boston Post Road, Port Chester, NY 10573, (914) 934-7629; paint from Kmart; water-based acrylic gloss from Janovic Plaza Paint and Wallpaper, 1150 Third Avenue, New York, NY 10021, (212) 772-1400.

PART THREE: How Much Is That Doggie in the Window? Picture Frames for Your Furry Friend

21. Dog Tag Picture Frame: picture frame from Lechters #513, Kohl's Shopping Center, Boston Post Road, Port Chester, NY 10573, (914) 934-7629.

22. A Frame Good Enough to Eat: dog biscuits (Milk-Bone) from Petco, 147 East 86th Street, New York, NY 10028, (212) 831-8001; frame from Lechters #513, Kohl's Shopping Center, Boston Post Road, Port Chester, NY 10573, (914) 934-7629.

23. Pet Silhouette: black paper from Kate's Paperie, 1282 Third Avenue, New York, NY 10021, (212) 941-9816; frames from an arts and crafts fair in Big Fork, Montana.

24. Playing Pooches Frame: frame from Lechters #513, Kohl's Shopping Center, Boston Post Road, Port Chester, NY 10573, (914) 934-7629.

25. All-About-Dogs Decoupage Picture Frame: frame from Lechters #513, Kohl's Shopping Center, Boston Post Road, Port Chester, NY 10573, (914) 934-7629; decoupage glaze from AI Freidman, 431 Boston Post Road, Port Chester, NY 10573, (914) 937-7351.

PART FOUR: Get on the Couch! Pooch Pillows and Other Stuffed Stuff

26. Pugs & Pillows: pug fabric from Lee Jofa, Cowtan & Taut, and Brunschwig & Fils (through decorators); trim from M & J Trimmings, 1008 Sixth Avenue (at 38th Street), New York, NY 10018, (212) 391-9072, www.mjtrim.com, and Paterson Silks, 156 East 86th Street, New York, NY 10023, (212) 722-4384 or (800) 522-5671.

27. Royal Pug Pillows: fabric from Lee Jofa (through decorators); background fabric from Paterson Silks, 156 East 86th Street,

New York, NY 10023, (212) 722-4384 or (800) 522-5671; trim from Regent Fabrics, 221 East 60th Street, New York, NY 10022, (212) 355-2039.

28. Hugo's Dog-Bone Button Pillow: fabric from Calico Corners, 1701 East Post Road, Westport, CT, (203) 254-7904; buttons from my own collection; trim from M & J Trimmings, 1008 Sixth Avenue (at 38th Street), New York, NY 10018, (212) 391-9072, www.mjtrim.com.

29. My Baby's Name in Bones: bone buttons from Michael's Arts and Crafts, 535 stores nationwide, www.michaels.com; pillow from The Company Store, (800) 285-3696, www.thecompanystore.com.

30. Scottie Pillowcase: fabric, buttons, and felt from Regent Fabrics, 221 East 60th Street, New York, NY 10022, (212) 355-2039.

31. Your-Dog-Here Pillow: fabric, buttons, and felt from Regent Fabrics, 221 East 60th Street, New York, NY 10022, (212) 355-2039.

32. Bundle Sachet: dog fabric from B&J Fabrics, 263 West 40th Street, New York, NY 10018, (212) 354-8150; lavender available at www.naturesproducts.com and www.countrycottageworks.com.

33. Shaped Sachet: dog fabric from B&J Fabrics, 263 West 40th Street, New York, NY 10018, (212) 354-8150; lavender available at www.naturesproducts.com and www.countrycottageworks.com.

34. Single Breed Sachet: dog fabric from B&J Fabrics, 263 West 40th Street, New York, NY 10018, (212) 354-8150; lavender available at www.naturesproducts.com and www.countrycottageworks.com.

35. Antique Dog-Button Pillow: buttons from Tender Buttons, 143 East 62nd Street, New York, NY 10021, (212) 758-7004, and M & J Buttons, 1000 Sixth Avenue, New York, NY 10018, (212) 391-6200, and www.buttons4u.com; pillow from The Company Store, (800) 285-3696, www.thecompanystore.com.

PART FIVE: Paper Training for Humans: Woofer Wrappings and Supplies

36. Sammy Stamps: cork, balsa wood, and foam from Michael's Arts and Crafts, 535 stores nationwide, www.michaels.com.

37. Bone and Hydrant Sponge Stamps: this craft uses only household items.

38. Who Let the Dogs Out? Stencils: blank stencil sheet from Michael's Arts and Crafts, 535 stores nationwide, www.michaels.com.

39. Tail-Waggingly Easy Invitation: card stock and markers from Staples Office Supplies, 1280 Lexington Avenue, New York, NY 10028, (212) 426-6190.

40. Woofer Wrapping Paper and Gift Tags: tempera paint from Office Max, 51-06 Northern Boulevard, Woodside, NY 11377, (718) 426-9055; ink pad from Kate's Paperie, 1282 Third Avenue, New York, NY 10021, (212) 941-9816.

41. "Pup-Up" Invitation or Greeting Card: construction paper from Michael's Arts and Crafts, 535 stores nationwide, www.michaels.com; card stock from Staples Office Supplies, 1280 Lexington Avenue, New York, NY 10028, (212) 426-6190.

42. Ode to Toupee Drink Coasters: colored paper from CVS Pharmacy, 342 East 23rd Street, New York, NY 10016, (212) 473-5750; laminate from Fromex Photo Systems, 1058 Third Avenue, New York, NY 10021, (212) 644-5678.

PART SIX: The Holidays Have Gone to the Dogs: Festive Fido Decorations

43. A Holiday Dog Breed Ornament: felt, ribbon, and bells from Regent Fabrics, 221 East 60th Street, New York, NY 10022, (212) 355-2039.

44. Too-Proud-to-Beg Bone Ornament: felt, ribbon, and buttons from Regent Fabrics, 221 East 60th Street, New York, NY 10022, (212) 355-2039.

45. Kennel Klub Kristmas Ornaments: cookie cutters from Kitchen Collectibles, 8901 J. Street, Suite 2, Omaha, NB 68127, (888) 593-2436 or (402) 597-0980, www.kitchencollectibles.com, and New York Cake Baking Distributors, Inc., 56 West 22nd Street, New York, NY 10010, (212) 675-2253; clay from Michael's Arts and Crafts, 535 stores nationwide, www.michaels.com; ribbon and gold thread from Daytona Braids and Trimmings, 251 West 39th Street, New York, NY 10018, (212) 354-1713.

46. Paw Print Ornament: Crayola molding clay from Michael's Arts and Crafts, 535 stores nationwide, www.michaels.com; gold thread from Daytona Braids and Trimmings, 251 West 39th Street, New York, NY 10018, (212) 354-1713.

PART SEVEN: Putting on the Pooch: For Dog Lovers on the Move

47. A-OK Dog Tag Earrings: dog tags from my vet; earring supplies from Michael's Arts and Crafts, 535 stores nationwide, www.michaels.com.

48. Dog-Button Earrings and Brooch: dog buttons from Michael's Arts and Crafts, 535 stores nationwide, www.michaels. com, and www.buttons4u.com, and Tender Buttons, 143 East 62nd Street, New York, NY 10021, (212) 758-7004, and M & J Buttons, 1000 Sixth Avenue, New York, NY 10018, (212) 391-6200; earring backs and bar pins from Michael's Arts and Crafts.

49. Sighing Dog Brooches: clay and bar pins from Michael's Arts and Crafts, 535 stores nationwide, www.michaels.com; ribbon from Daytona Braids and Trimmings, 251 West 39th Street, New York, NY 10018, (212) 354-1713.

50. Dog-Chase Garden Hat: garden hat from Orva Hosiery Store, 155 East 86th Street, New York, NY 10028, (212) 369-3448.

Acknowledgments

I would like to thank the following people who helped me and my book on our path to being published: Kelly Colquitt, who took my hand at the starting gates and led me in the right direction; Amye Dyer, who liked the book even though she's not a dog lover (gasp!); Georg Brewer, who made these crafts a terrific visual experience; Dorsey Mills, who took me and the Fido Finial under her wing; Steve Cohen, who always seems to be there for me, wherever there may be; Caitlin Blasdell, who has offered me sound advice along the way; Goss and Keeks, for giving me my first dog and endless love and support; Scout, who went without long walks so I could work; and lastly Ted, who, whenever he found me excessively whining and running after my tail, didn't drop me off at the nearest pound.

Index

Italic page references denote illustrations.

Affenpinscher, 148
Afghan Hound, 9, 148
Airedale Terrier, 132, 147, *149*
Akita, 16, 147, *149*, *161*
Alaskan Malamute, 38, 147, *149*, *161*
All-About-Dogs Decoupage Picture Frame, 67–68
American Eskimo Dog, 148
American Foxhound, 148
American Kennel Club: library of, 143; list of popular breeds, 147–48
American Staffordshire Terrier, 147
American Water Spaniel, 148
Anatolian Shepherd Dog, 148
Antique Dog-Button Pillow, 98–99
A-OK Dog Tag Earrings, 137–38
ASPCA, 45, 105
Australian Cattle Dog, 147
Australian Shepherd, 6, 147, *149*, *161*
Australian Terrier, 148

bales, 25–26
Basenji, 10, 147
Basset Hound, 4, 10, 53, 147, *150*, *161*
Beagle, 58, 113, 147, *150*, *161*

Beardie Collie, 148
Bedlington Terrier, 148
Belgian Malinois, 148
Belgian Sheepdog, 148
Belgian Tervuren, 148
Bernese Mountain Dog, 34, 147
Best-in-Show Lazy Susan, 51–53
Bichon Frise, 10, 32, 34, 110, 112, 122, 127, 144, 147, *150*, *161*
birthday parties for dogs, 116
Black and Tan Coonhound, 148
Bloodhound, 147
Bobnams & Brooks, 20
Bobtail, 19
Bone and Hydrant Sponge Stamps, 106–7, 113
Bone Bales, 25–26
Bone Doormat, 6
Border Collie, 147
Border Terrier, 148
Borzoi, 9, 148
Boston Terrier, 119, 147, *150*
Bouvier des Flandres, 147
Boxer, 24, 147, *150*, *161*
Briard, 148
Brittany, 9, 147, *150*, *161*
brooches, 141–43
Brussels Griffon, 77, 147, *161*
Bulldog, 19, 32, 122, 147, *151*, *162*

Bullmastiff, 147
Bull Terrier, 147
Bundle Sachet, 93–94
Burgh, Henry, 45
buttons, 98

Cairn Terrier, 145, 147, *151*, *162*
Canaan Dog, 148
candle holders, 42–45
Cardigan Welsh Corgi, 53, 147, *162*
Cavalier King Charles Spaniel, 21, 147, *162*
Chesapeake Bay Retriever, 6, 147, *151*, *162*
Chihuahua, 35, 61, 147, *151*, *162*
Chinese Crested, 147
Chinese Shar-Pei, 147
Chow Chow, 10, 45, 147, *151*, *162*
Clay Bone Pitcher Protectors, 50
Clumber Spaniel, 148
coasters, 120–22
Cocker Spaniel, 12, 147, *151*, *162*
Collie, 10, 132, 147, *152*, *162*
Corgi, *152*
corkboards, 22–24
Crufts Dog Show, 53
Curly-Coated Retriever, 148

Dachshund, 4, 35, 64, 122, 143, 145, 147, *152, 163*
Dalmatian, 31, 147, *152, 163*
Dandie Dinmont Terrier, 148
decoupage, 20–24, 25, 65, 67–68
Doberman Pinscher, 105, 147, *152, 163*
"dog," meanings of the word, 81
dog art, 20, 21
dog biscuits, 59–60
Dog-Button Earrings and Brooch, 139–40
Dog-Chase Garden Hat, 144–45
Dog Phrase Napkin Rings, 37–38
Dog Run Corkboard, 22–24
dogs: fertility of, 58, 81; in history, 74, 87, 134, 145; love of, *xv*; naming, 42, 82, 103; popular breeds, 31, 72, 147–48, 149; proverbs and phrases about, 37–38; reincarnation as, 36; that author has known, *xii, xv,* 19, 22, 39, 42, 57, 61, 78, 82, 103, 112, 116, 120, 130, 133, 144
dog shows, 51, 53
Dogs-in-Art Tissue Box Cover, 20–21
Dog Tag Picture Frame, 57–58
dog tags, 137
doormats, 5–6

earrings, 137–40
English Bulldog, 34
English Cocker Spaniel, 147
English Foxhound, 148
English Setter, 148
English Springer Spaniel, 4, 9, 139, 147, *152, 163*
English Toy Spaniel, 148
exercise, 13

Fetch, Run, Catch, Play! Tic-Tac-Toe Board, 13–14
Fido Finials, 3–4
Field Spaniel, 148
finials, 3–4
Finnish Spitz, 148
Flat-Coated Retriever, 148
A Frame Good Enough to Eat, 59–60
French Bulldog, 34, 147

game boards, 13–14
German Pinscher, 105

German Shepherd, 19, 31, 147, *153, 163*
German Shorthaired Pointer, 147
German Wirehaired Pointer, 147
Giant Schnauzer, 147
gift tags, 113–15
Give-a-Dog-a-Bone Place Mats, 35–36
Golden Retriever, 14, 31, 105, 147, *153, 163*
Gordon Setter, 147
Great Dane, 99, 147, *153, 163*
Greater Swiss Mountain Dog, 148
Great Pyrenees, 133, 147, *153, 163*
Great Swiss Sennehund (Swissy), 34
greeting cards, 116–19
Greyhound, 99, 105, 148

Harrier, 148
hats, 144–45
Havanese, 148
Hecht, Irene, 133
Holiday Dog Breed Ornament, 125–27
Hugo's Dog-Bone Button Pillow, 78–81
Husky, 96, *153, 163*

Ibizan Hound, 148
In the Company of Dogs, 26
invitations, 116–19
Irish Setter, 105, 147
Irish Terrier, 148
Irish Water Spaniel, 148
Irish Wolfhound, 148
Italian Greyhound, 10, 147

Jack Russell Terrier, 107, 147, *153, 164*
Japanese Chin, 147
Joan Peck Fine Paintings, 21

Kanine Key Hooks, 17–18
Keeshond, 147
Kennel Klub Kristmas Ornaments, 130–32
Kerry Blue Terrier, 148
key hooks, 17–19
Komondor, 148
Kuvasz, 148

Labrador Retriever, 10, 31, 35, 147, *154, 164*
Lakeland Terrier, 148
lampshade finials, 3–4

Lassie (of the movies), 132
lazy Susans, 51–53
leash, dog on, 19
Leash (club), 140
Lhasa Apso, 81, 147, *154, 164*
licking, 31
Lowchen, 148
Lucky's Luminary, 42–45
luminaries, 42–45
Lyin' Dog Place Card Holders, 29–31

magnets, 46–48
Maltese, 88, 91, 147, *154*
Manchester Terrier, 105, 148
Mastiff, 138, 147, *154*
message board, 7–9
Miniature Bull Terrier, 148
Miniature Pinscher, 109, 147, *154, 164*
Miniature Schnauzer, 147
Mug-for-Me Decoupage Plates, 32–34
My Baby's Name in Bones, 82–83

napkin rings, 37–38
napkins, 39–41
Newfoundland, 115, 147, *164*
No-Drool Napkins, 39–41
Norfolk Terrier, 107, 148, *164*
Norwegian Elkhound, 147
Norwich Terrier, 10, 107, 148

Ode to Toupee Drink Coasters, 120–22
Old English Sheepdog, 19, 53, 147, *164*
ornaments, 125–34
Otterhound, 148
Our Doghouse Placard, 15–16

Paper Using Bone and Hydrant Sponge Stamps, 113–14
Paper Using Sammy Stamps, 115
Papillon, 138, 147, *154, 164*
Paw Print Magnets, 46–48
Paw Print Ornament, 133–34
paws, 48
Pekingese, 81, 147, *155, 164*
Pembroke Welsh Corgi, 19, 147
Petit Basset Griffon Vendeen, 148
Pet Silhouette, 61–64
Pharaoh Hound, 148
picture frames, 57–68
pillows, 71–91

pitcher covers, 49–50
placards, 15–16
place card holders, 29–31
place mats, 35–36
plates, 32–34
Playing Pooches Frame, 65–66
Plott Coonhound, 148
Pointer, 16, 61, 148, *155*, *165*
Polish Lowland Sheepdog, 148
Pomeranian, 10, 143, 145, 147, *155*, *165*
Poochie-Poo Pitcher Protector, 49–50
Poodle, 64, 122, 147, *155*
Pop-Up Dog Bowl Invitation, 119
Portuguese Water Dog, 147
Pug, 25, 34, 72, 147, *155*
Pugs & Pillows, 72–74
Puli, 148
"Pup-Up" Invitation or Greeting Card, 116–18

Retriever, 14
Retriever Message Board, 7–9
Rhodesian Ridgeback, 147
Rin Tin Tin, 19
Rottweiler, 105, 133, 147, *155*, *165*
Royal Pug Pillows, 75–77

sachets, 92–99
Saint Bernard, 41, 147, *156*, *165*
St. John's Water Dogs, 35
Saluki, 9, 148
Sammy Stamps, 103–5, 115
Samoyed, 147
Schipperke, 147
Schnauzer, 132, *156*, *165*

Scottie Pillowcase, 84–87
Scottish Deerhound, 148
Scottish Terrier, 61, 64, 84, 87, 127, 147, *156*
Scout (author's dog), *xii*, 19, 22, 39, 42, 57, 61, 78, 82, 112, 116, 130, 133, 144
Sealyham Terrier, 148
Shaped Sachet, 95
Shar-Pei, 45, 147, *156*, *165*
shelters, 45
Shetland Sheepdog (Shelties), 48, 147, *156*, *165*
Shiba Inu, 147
Shih Tzu, 60, 147, *156*, *165*
Siberian Husky, 94, 147, *153*, *163*
Sighing Dog Brooch, 141–43
silhouettes, 61–64
Silky Terrier, 147
Single Breed Sachet, 96–97
Skye Terrier, 148
sleep, dogs', 16
smell (sense of), 41
Smooth Fox Terrier, 148
Soft Coated Wheaten Terrier, 147
Spaniels, 139
Spinone Italiano, 148
Springer Spaniel, 10
Staffordshire Bull Terrier, 148
stamps, 103–7
Standard Schnauzer, 148
Stenciled Bone Bale, 26
stencils, 108–11
Sussex Spaniel, 148
Swiss Mountain Dogs, 34

Tail-Waggingly Easy Invitation, 110–11

tassels, decorative, 10–12
Tassel That Wags the Dog, 10–12
Terrier, 34, 107
Tibetan Spaniel, 148
Tibetan Terrier, 42, 148
tissue box covers, 20–21
Too-Proud-to-Beg Bone Ornament, 128
Toy Spaniel, 21
tracings of popular breeds, 149
Tweed Water Spaniel, 14
Two-Dog Key Hook, 19

veterinarians, 57, 137, 138
Vizsla, 10, 109, 147, *157*, *165*

war dogs, 109, 138
Washington, George, 31
Wegman, William, 53
Weimaraner, 53, 105, 147, *157*, *166*
Welsh Springer Spaniel, 148
Welsh Terrier, 148
West Highland White Terrier (Westie), 35, 147, *157*
Westminster Kennel Club Dog Show, 20, 51, 53, 107
Whippet, 12, 147
William Doyle Gallery, 20
William Secord Gallery, 21
Wire Fox Terrier, 147
Wirehaired Pointing Griffon, 148
Woofer Wrapping Paper and Gift Tags, 113–15
wrapping paper, 113–15

Yorkshire Terrier, 132, 147, *157*, *166*
Your-Dog-Here Pillow, 88–91